The HOMEMADE WORKSHOP

Build Your Own
Woodworking Machines & Jigs

James Hamilton

POPULAR WOODWORKING BOOKS

Cincinnati, Ohio
popularwoodworking.com

Contents

CHAPTER 1 · PAGE 9

Sliding-top Router Table
The unique sliding top makes joinery tasks safe and easy.

CHAPTER 2 · PAGE 19

Multi-function Router Lift
Make precise adjustments from above, or use the lift itself as a fully functional mini table.

CHAPTER 3 · PAGE 31

Micro-adjustible Router Table Fence
The lead screw positioner enables this fence to do more than any homemade version ever has.

CHAPTER 4 · PAGE 39

Benchtop Jigsaw
Turn a hand-held power tool into a benchtop machine that can do things a band saw can't.

CHAPTER 5 · PAGE 49

Multi-function Downdraft Table
Keep the dust out of your lungs while sanding, and use the T-tracks for countless workholding applications.

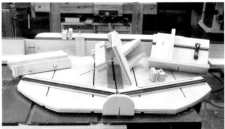

About StumpyNubs.com

The Homemade Workshop is much bigger than a single book. This is just a starting point: 12 projects to demonstrate what's possible. But if you really want to transform your workshop you'll want to go far beyond a few homemade tools. You'll need more ideas, more tips and tricks, more inspiration – more of everything. Well, we've got you covered. On our website you'll find a regular supply of woodworking articles, project plans and video podcasts, all designed to help you improve your workshop and skill set. We focus on regular woodworkers with limited budgets. But this isn't your typical "let's build another birdhouse" website. Our goal is to inspire you to do greater things through what we call "infotainment." It's a mix of tips, tricks, techniques, unique projects and a healthy dose of dumb jokes.

STAY UP TO DATE AND LEARN NEW THINGS WITH 'BEHIND THE SAWDUST'

We developed this "news style" show to help you stay up to date with the latest in the woodworking world. But it isn't just about news. We highlight tips and tricks from the pros, new tools that you may want to check out (or avoid), and we mix in a healthy dose of humor. It's designed to make you feel like you're enjoying the morning paper with various sections from news to editorial, and even a projects gallery to give you new ideas. We share highlights from all of

the woodworking journals, blogs and more – the best and most useful information. New episodes are released weekly and are about 5-7 minutes in length. This is a great show for those who simply don't have the time to sort through all of the great content available to woodworkers these days. You'll learn something new in every episode, and your skills and knowledge of the craft will grow.

GET MORE IN DEPTH WITH 'THE STUMPY NUBS WORKSHOP' VLOG

This weekly video podcast is where we test out new ideas. We build jigs and shop improvements, we try out new tools and figure out ways to make our shops better. All of the machines in this book and many others were developed on these episodes, and we're always working on something new. During 2015 we outfitted two vastly different workshops on the show, creating new ways to utilize small spaces efficiently. We review tools in greater depth on this show, and we demonstrate techniques that you can use on your own projects. This series is about getting the most out of your workshop and is full of good ideas. New episodes are released about once a week and the format is convenient to watch in your free time!

PUT YOUR HOMEMADE TOOLS TO WORK WITH 'THE HOMEMADE WORKSHOP'

Building your own router table or workbench is one thing, but is a completely homemade workshop possible? Absolutely it is! In fact, that's just what we've done! In 2015 we launched an all new online woodworking show called "The Homemade Workshop." Filmed in a small workspace full of tools that we designed and built ourselves, we make small boxes, large cabinets and everything in between. The show is designed to entertain and inform, with woodworking tips and tricks and unique project designs, but it also serves to demonstrate that anything is possible with inexpensive homemade machines. New episodes are released every week or so and typically run from 20 minutes to a half hour. Even if your shop is full of store-bought machines, you'll enjoy the projects we build on this show!

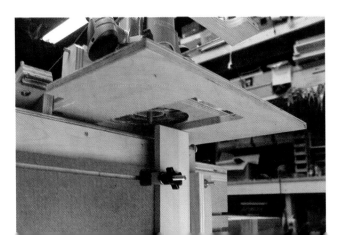

LEARN HAND-TOOL WOODWORKING WITH 'THE OLD-TIMEY WORKSHOP'

This is one of our most popular video series! Whether we're building an 18th century workbench or just talking about a long forgotten tool, every episode takes you back to the old days. We use our large collection of antique woodworking tools to build projects, demonstrate techniques and preserve a fading way of life. New episodes are released periodically and this is a great series for woodworkers of all skill levels, even those who have never considered working without electricity.

VISIT OUR LIBRARY OF PROJECT PLANS AND TUTORIALS

Many of the projects we build on our various online woodworking shows are also available as downloadable plans. Most of these plans include far more than dimensioned drawings. We walk you through the entire project with step-by-step instructions, photographs, cutlists and more. From homemade woodworking machines to unique projects of our own design, this constantly expanding library is a fantastic resource for woodworkers looking for a new challenge or just new ideas. You can visit the current collection at stumpynubs.com/homemade-tools.html.

About the Author

A lot of people wonder about a guy who goes by the name "Stumpy Nubs." Is he missing a few fingers? A few marbles? When asked, I always raise my hands to display 10 intact digits, and I flash a smile somewhere between friendly and "he's not all there, is he?" Because you have to be a little crazy to do what I do. I'm a full-time woodworker who rarely sells his woodwork. Sure, I make everything from boxes and birdhouses to cabinets and furniture. And I'm told that I do it very well – but I don't build furniture for a living.

I build workshops. I teach people how to create a woodworking wonderland with little more than a small space and a smaller budget. I show regular woodworkers how a basement, garage, shed or patio can become a fully functional furniture factory (or just a laid-back, sawdust-on-the-floor man-cave to wile away a weekend). I'm a self-taught tool expert, engineer, writer, teacher and video producer. But I wasn't always living the dream. I spent 20 years running a family business while my woodworking interests were relegated to an hour here and there on the weekends while I dreamt of getting some real shop time in somewhere between retirement and death.

But you can't keep a woodworker down for long. In 2008 I went into woodworking full time, creating a weekly Internet woodworking show that focused on the workshop itself. From that small beginning we've grown into one of the most popular multi-media woodworking resources in the industry. We now produce three different Internet woodworking shows. I've designed dozens of unique jigs and tools, and I've been honored to contribute articles, blogs, classes and educational content for some of the most respected institutions in our craft. That's a real accomplishment for a nobody with a dumb nickname, and not a day goes by that I don't think about those who have helped me along the way.

Charles Neil, the finest woodworker I've even known, has mentored me even though I called him a hillbilly. The Rockler Woodworking and Hardware family sponsored us when we had little more than a few thousand viewers. Popular Woodworking Books took a chance on me when they offered to publish my first book. And my father, whom viewers of our show know as "Mustache Mike," has humbly played the role of my "sidekick" since the beginning. It's been a great ride, and the best part is, we're just getting started!

Introduction

When I put together my first workshop, I couldn't afford a band saw. Now, I could have scrimped and saved, maybe skipped a few trips to the buffet until I gathered the funds together for a good used model. But I come from a long line of tinkerers. My great grandfather was an iron worker. My grandfather was a well driller. When they had a problem, they built their own solution out of the materials they were familiar with (and a little bit of duct tape). So I wondered, was it really possible to build my own band saw?

It didn't take me long to find my answer. It turns out that homemade woodworking machines used to be quite popular. In the days before moderately priced imports, tools were very expensive. So innovative woodworkers began making their own. One of my favorites was found in an old issue of *Popular Mechanics* magazine. It was a detailed plan for a band saw built from steel pipe fittings. Later I learned that at least one company (Gilliom Manufacturing under the name "Gil-Bilt") had for years manufactured bits of hardware that could be combined with wood to create all sorts of woodworking machines. I found that, not only was it possible to make my own tools, but that people had been doing it for decades!

That is until the 1980s. The decade of stonewashed jeans and hair bands also saw an influx of imports from the Asian markets. Suddenly a new band saw could be had for half the price as before. The homemade tool revolution dwindled as quickly as Don Johnson's career after "Miami Vice." But enough with the 80s pop culture references; let's get to the heart of the matter. These days homemade woodworking tools are making a comeback. But it isn't all about saving a few bucks.

WHY BUILD YOUR OWN TOOLS?

More Features

I feel like the tool manufacturers have let us down. They've been pumping out the same old stuff for years with few new innovations. There are some exceptions, of course. But many of the most common machines haven't changed in generations. Let's stick with the band saw as an example. Today's new models look very much like the old belt-driven machines in museums. Meanwhile a guy named Bell invented a box with a microphone that evolved from the candlestick telephone to party lines, touch-tone dials, cordless phones, cell phones and now Internet video connections – and we're still using the same band saw design!

Where's the built-in sliding crosscut table, the integrated dust collection that actually collects dust, or the space-saving design that gives you more than 14" of throat depth without requiring a 10' machine with giant wheels? My homemade version has all of those features, and that's just a start.

You see, when you build it yourself, you get to decide what features are important to you. With a little thought (along with some help from this book and the content at stumpynubs. com) you can make machines that are light years ahead of those available in stores.

Less Cost

Building your own woodworking machines is a great way to save money, if you're into that sort of thing. (Which I am.)

Because the band saw example has been working for us so well, let's consider it again. I am the proud owner of a 1hp, 14" band saw that is considered a fairly "premium" model. It cost me $1,000. You can buy less expensive saws, but not with the features that come in this price range. I also own a homemade saw of my own design. It has all of the features that my $1,000 saw has, plus a lot more. It cost me about $100 to build, including a used motor. But that doesn't tell the whole story. My homemade saw has 24" of capacity. A 24" band saw on the commercial market will cost you several thousand dollars more.

I also have a homemade horizontal router, a drum sander, a router joinery machine, a dovetail machine and all sorts of other machinery that's rarely ever found in a small shop, because the commercial versions are far beyond the financial means of the average woodworker. My shop is vastly better equipped than many professional shops for one simple reason: I made my own tools.

Greater Access

We finance the work we do, in part, through the sale of plans and building instructions for the machines I design (stumpy nubs.com/homemade-tools.html).

Thousands of woodworkers have built these machines, which is something I take a great deal of pride in. But the best part of my job is reading email from woodworkers who live in areas where woodworking machinery is either difficult to find or prohibitively expensive to import. Many in Europe, Africa and Asia have found that building their own machines is the only way they could ever hope to own some of the tools that others find easy to acquire.

That band saw that cost $1,000 in the United States is two or three times that cost in some countries. Others simply can't find a commercial version for sale at all. While availability isn't an issue for everyone, for some it is a big reason to build their own tools.

Bragging Rights

My neighbor once came to my shop to show me a cutting board he'd made. He was very proud of his work, as everybody is when they create something with their own hands. I complimented him and chatted about it until he mentioned that he still had to finish the sanding. Being a good neighbor, I offered to do it for him, flipping on my homemade drum sander. His jaw dropped as I fed it through, making a point to adjust every knob and crank as if it were H.G. Wells' time machine. You may think me cruel to show him up like that, but you don't know my neighbor.

The first thing every woodworker should learn is this: Nothing impresses your friends, and the ladies, like homemade machines. Give your buddies a quick tour of your shop and you'll be master of the woodworking universe forever! But homemade machines aren't just about impressing your friends. Imagine the satisfaction you get when you finish a project.

Now imagine making that project with tools you also made yourself! It's a challenge, but with the step-by-step instructions in this book you'll be amazed at what you can accomplish. And that feeling will return every time you use your new machine.

DON'T BE INTIMIDATED!

I find that a lot of people are intimidated by the idea of building something so complex as a homemade woodworking machine. And I will admit that designing an accurate and fully functional tool can be a difficult task. But I've done all of that work for you! The projects in this book have been built, tested, rebuilt and retested, the designs simplified and refined, all with you in mind. When I build a machine, the first thing I ask myself is, how will "Joe Woodworker" down the street (or across the country) be able to build it with basic tools and readily available hardware. A great deal of effort goes into creating easy-to-follow, step-by-step instructions complete with photos and tips so that anyone can reproduce the projects.

This book is designed with all woodworkers in mind, so you'll find a project that interests you no matter what sort of shop you have. But the projects are organized with the small shop woodworker especially in mind.

Because the router is one of the most important yet most under-utilized tools in the shop, the first three projects are focused on getting more out of yours. You'll build a unique router table, a lift and a fence that will turn your router into the powerhouse of your workshop. After that, you'll find some new machines that will take your shop to the next level, includ-

WHAT DO YOU NEED TO GET STARTED?

These projects are designed to be built with basic tools and woodworking skills. But you will need a few things:

- **PATIENCE**: The most important thing is to take your time. Make your cuts straight and precise, assemble the parts with care, and double-check everything before applying any glue or fasteners. Spend some time checking your tools for proper alignment, too. It's not about skill; it's about "measuring twice, cutting once" as they say.

- **TABLE SAW**: While it is possible to make straight, accurate cuts with a circular saw and a guide, a table saw will make your work a lot easier. You don't need an expensive saw; just be sure the fence is parallel to the blade.

- **DRILL PRESS**: Some of these projects require holes to be bored perfectly perpendicular to the work piece. An inexpensive drill press is the best tool for the job, but you could also use a hand-held drilling jig.

- **OPTIONAL TOOLS**: A pneumatic brad nailer will really speed things up by reducing clamping time. A basic router table is also a big help, so you may want to build that project first if you don't have one. The workstation project utilizes a pocket hole jig, but there are ways to get around that. Everything else can be accomplished with basic tools you likely already own.

ing a jigsaw, a downdraft dust collection table, a shop vacuum cyclone and a table saw crosscut sled with joinery attachments.

Next, we'll move on to a pair of machines that will represent a serious upgrade for most shops: a drum sander and a 24" band saw.

Finally we'll turn to the most important tool in your shop – the table saw. We'll make a micro-adjustable fence, a sliding table attachment, and a workstation that's designed to bring many of the projects together into one 4' x 8' footprint. I'll walk you through each project step by step and you'll find free additional content on stumpynubs.com. So what are you waiting for? Let's build some tools!

Sliding-top Router Table

Next to the table saw, the router table is the most important "machine" in the workshop. It may sound strange to call it a "machine." After all, isn't it just a table with a router mounted beneath? Not in my shop! I'm tired of ordinary router tables that do little more than hold my router upside down while it does all the work! The table shouldn't be a mere accessory, it should be a complete package that transforms the router into a lean, mean woodworking machine. That's what I set out to achieve with this design.

Homemade router tables are a dime a dozen, but there's never been one quite like this. It borrows an idea that's been used on European table saws for years — the sliding table. Sliding tables make crosscuts safer and more accurate, and they can open up a whole new world of possibilities when applied to the router table. Consider the common task of routing the end of a rail for a frame-and-panel door. This is too dangerous to be accomplished

freehand so most cabinetmakers use a miter gauge or a coping sled. But with this design you need only clamp it to the table itself using the built-in T-tracks and removable fence. The entire front of the table moves past the cutter, securely carrying the workpiece with it. It's more accurate, it's safer, and it's just the beginning of what can be accomplished with this unique innovation in homemade router table design!

When used in conjunction with your router lift (or the homemade lift we'll build in Chapter 2) and the unique fence we build in Chapter 3, this sliding-top design enables your router to cut complex dovetails, finger joints, tenons and a lot more. There's plenty of storage for bits and accessories with the six drawers. Plus it's heavy enough to dampen vibration, yet compact enough to sit on a benchtop.

In this chapter I'll help you build your own sliding router table and show you how to mount your lift or router plate. Let's get started.

A homemade router table with a unique sliding top that makes it easy and safe to do a whole host of joinery operations!

Sliding-top Router Table

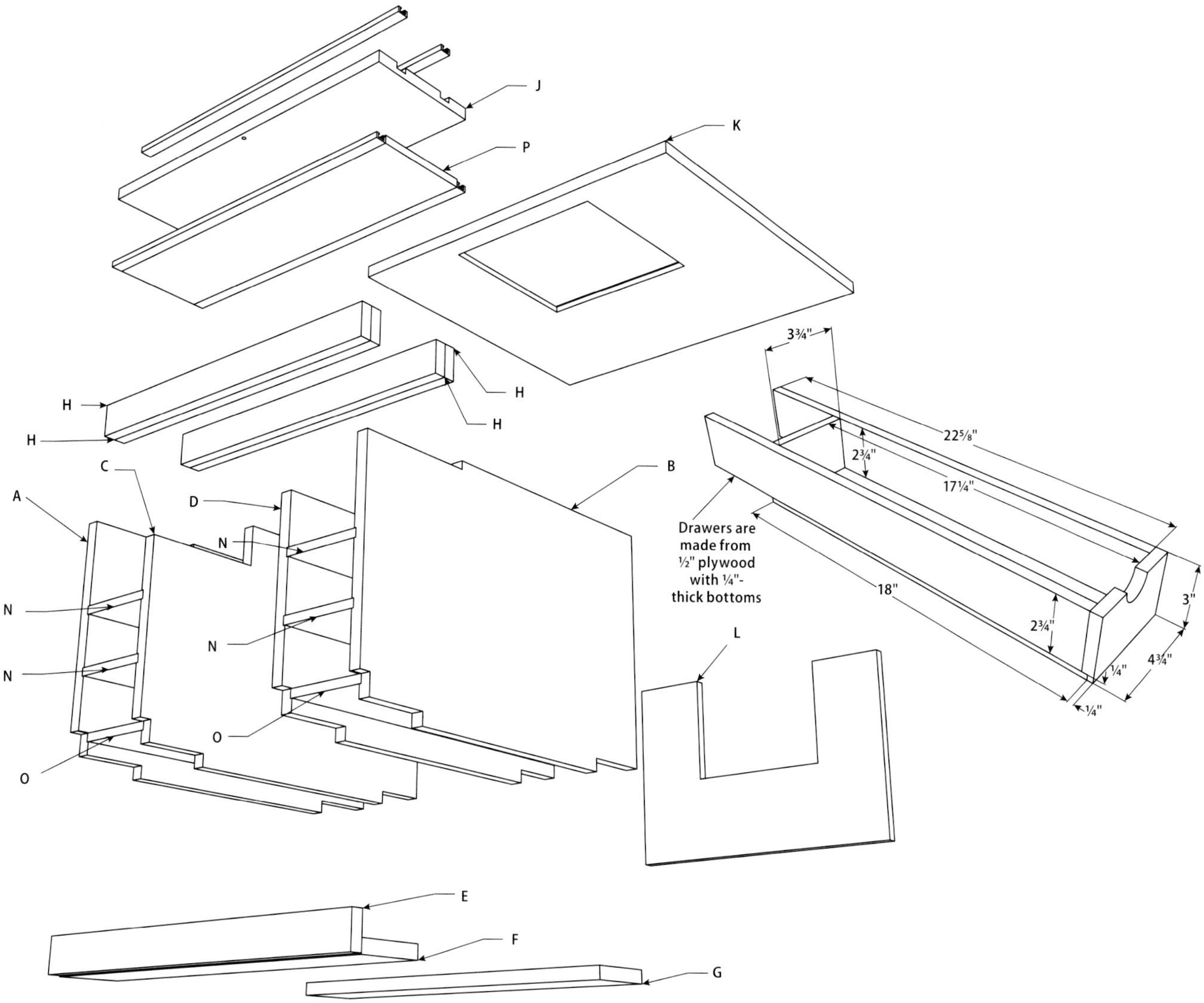
J
K
P
H
H
H
H
C
A
D
B
N
N
N
N
O
O
L
E
F
G
Drawers are made from ½" plywood with ¼"-thick bottoms
3¾"
22⅝"
2¾"
17¼"
18"
3"
2¾"
4¾"
¼"
¼"

Materials List

QTY	PART	REFERENCE	DIMENSIONS	STOCK
2	Outer side panels	A & B	23⅞" x 14⅞"	¾" plywood
2	Inner side panels	C & D	23⅛" x 14⅞"	¾" plywood
1	Front box stretcher	E	23½" x 2"	¾" plywood
2	Bottom box stretchers	F & G	23½" x 4"	¾" plywood
4	Carriage support rails	H	22" x 2"	¾" plywood
1	Upper carriage panel	J	23½" x 7½"	¾" plywood
1	Top panel	K	23½" x 22"	¾" plywood
1	Back panel	L	14⅛" x 22"	¾" plywood
6	Drawer fronts	M	3" x 4¾"	¾" plywood
4	Upper drawer shelves	N	23⅛" x 5⅛"	½" plywood
2	Lower drawer shelves	O	23⅜" x 5⅛"	½" plywood
1	Lower carriage panel	P	23½" x 6"	½" plywood
12	Drawer sides	Q	22⅝" x 2¾"	½" plywood
6	Drawer backs	R	2¾" x 3¾"	½" plywood
6	Drawer bottoms	S	4¾" x 18"	¼" plywood

Additional Hardware

4	2' lengths of aluminum T-track
1	¼" T-track nut
2	¼" T-track bolts, 2" long
2	¼" wing nuts
1	¼" flat-head machine screw, 1½" long

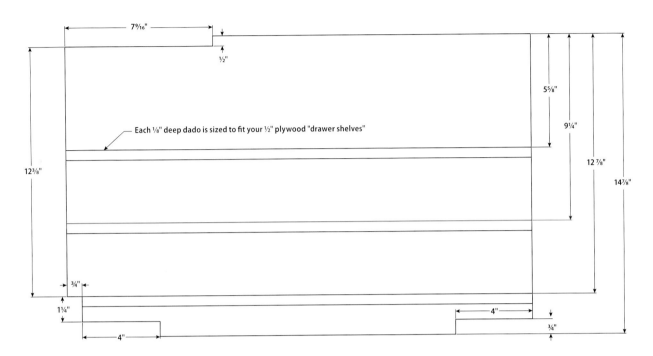

Outer side panels (A&B)
You must make two of these. Cut the dados on opposite sides of each so that they are mirror images of each other.

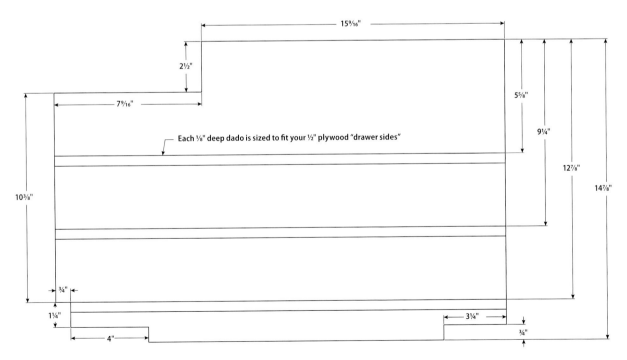

Inner side panels (C&D)
You must make two of these. Cut the dados on opposite sides of each so that they are mirror images of each other.

Figure 1

PART ONE: THE DRAWER BANKS

STEP 1: Lay out the notches that must be cut in the edges of the outer (A and B) and inner (C and D) side panels (see dimensioned diagrams). The best way to cut these is with a band saw, but a jigsaw will work, too. Take your time and be sure your cuts are clean and on the layout lines. The two longer panels will be identical to each other at this stage. The two shorter panels will likewise be identical to each other, but it's best to lay out each panel with a ruler and pencil individually **(Figure 1)** rather than cutting one panel then tracing around it to transfer the lines to the matching panel. The care you put into these cuts will be critical to proper operation of the table once it is completed.

STEP 2: As you lay out your dados on the side panels, keep in mind that each outer panel will have a corresponding inner panel that will be a mirror image of it. This means the dados will be cut on one side of outer panel A, and on the mating side of inner panel C; likewise with panels B and D **(Figure 2)**. Each of the dados are ⅛" deep. The width depends on the thickness of your ½" plywood stock as some sheet goods may vary in thickness. If you don't have a table saw dado set, use a router and a straightedge guide.

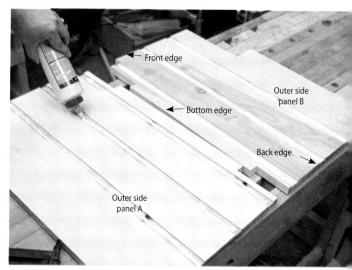
Figure 2

STEP 3: Lay the outer side panels (A and B) flat on the bench, dado side up. (Remember, the outer side panels are slightly wider than the inner panels.) Glue a lower shelf (O) in the bottom dado of each panel. The shelves are shorter than the panels are wide, so they must be positioned properly. These two lower shelves should be flush with the notch in the front edge of the panel

STEP 4: Next glue upper shelves (N) in the remaining dados **(Figure 3)**. These also sit flush with the front edge of the side panels. Place the inner side panels (C and D) on top, aligning the shelves in the corresponding dados **(Figure 4)**. Be sure everything is square before clamping to dry or securing with brad nails. You will now have two drawer banks that are mirror images of each other **(Figure 5)**.

Figure 3

STEP 5: Set your two drawer banks on the bench side by side with the bottoms (the side with notches in both the front and back corners) facing up. Be sure the inner panels of each drawer bank are facing each other. Place the bottom stretchers (F and G) into the notches, sliding the drawer banks apart so they fit properly. Make sure the drawer banks are parallel to each other, then use screws to fasten the stretchers in place **(Figure 6)**. Then use screws to attach the front stretcher (E) into the notch on the front of the drawer banks **(Figure 7)**.

Label Your Parts!

All of these parts can get mixed up in a hurry! As you cut each one to size, use a pencil to label them with the letters included in the cutlist. It's also a good idea to mark the top edge and outer face of the major pieces.

Shmudy Nubs Woodworking

PRO TIP

Figure 4

Figure 5

Figure 6

Figure 7

STEP 6: Flip the entire assembly over and locate your four carriage rails (H). Glue them together into two sandwiches, turning your four rails into two thicker rails. You will recall that the two inner side panels of your drawer banks have large notches cut in the top. That's where these two rails fit, spanning the two banks. Position one against the front edge of the notches and the other against the rear edges. The ends of the rails should butt up against the inside of the outer side panels. You will secure them in place with screws driven through the outer side panels and into the ends of the two rails **(Figure 8)**. You may also wish to drive screws through the back rail into the edges of the two inner side panels. Be certain that both rails are parallel to each other and to the top of the two drawer banks before you fasten them in place. This is critical!

Figure 8

STEP 7: Install the back panel (L) with screws on the back of the two drawer banks. If you are not planning on installing my homemade router lift with built-in lower dust collection, you should cut a hole in the back panel to fit your dust collection fittings. If you are installing my router lift, cut a large opening in the back panel so you can reach your arm inside to attach a dust collection hose directly to the lift.

You Need a Good Pilot

Never drive a screw without first drilling a pilot hole, especially in the edge of plywood! Not only will it prevent splitting, but it will prevent the screws from wandering as they make their way between the plies. Properly positioned pilot holes are also critical when installing the T-tracks in this and other projects in this book.

Stumpy Nubs Woodworking

PRO TIP

PART TWO: THE TOP

NOTE: The next few steps must be completed with care, checking that each part is properly aligned as it is installed. Use the front edge of your cabinet as a reference. Everything must be parallel to that edge.

STEP 8: Cut two lengths of T-track to 23½" long. Attach one on top of the front carriage rail, right along the front edge **(Figure 9)**. Be sure to drill properly centered pilot holes or you may throw your track out of alignment when you drive the screws.

STEP 9: Place the lower carriage panel (P) on top of the rails, against the front T-track. Install a second T-track along the back edge of that panel, fastening it to the rail beneath **(Figure 10)**.

STEP 10: Lay your top panel (K) on top of the drawer banks. Position its front edge flush with the top of the notches above your T-track. Run a combination square down the edge of the panel to ensure that it is perfectly parallel to the front edge of the cabinet **(Figure 11)**, then fasten the top panel down with countersunk screws. Use four along the front and rear edges, and one or two on each side.

STEP 11: Cut a pair of dados into the upper carriage panel to fit two pieces of T-track, one about 1½" from the front edge and the other the same distance from the rear edge. The depth and width of your dados will depend on your T-track, but most are ⅝" wide and ⅜" deep.

Figure 9

Figure 10

Figure 11

Figure 12

Figure 13

STEP 12: Position the upper carriage panel over the lower carriage panel and the T-track you previously mounted. Use a couple of washers to achieve a consistent gap between the edge of the upper carriage panel and the cabinet's top panel (**Figure 12**), then drive countersunk screws down through the upper carriage panel and into the panel below it, securing the two together.

STEP 13: Install the T-track in the dados of your newly assembled carriage (**Figure 13**).

STEP 14: With the carriage back in place, measure from the front edge to the center of the front T-track beneath (**Figure 14**). Transfer that measurement to the center of the carriage's front edge and bore a ¼" countersunk hole. Install a short flat-head machine screw and a T-nut to serve as a lock to keep the carriage from moving when you don't need it to (**Figure 15**).

Figure 14

Figure 15

PART THREE: THE DRAWERS

STEP 15: Locate all six of your drawer fronts (M). Raise your table saw blade or dado set ½" and cut a ¼"-wide rabbet along the bottom edge of each **(Figure 16)**. You may also wish to bore a hole in each front for a finger hold unless you plan on installing knobs **(Figure 17)**.

STEP 16: Fasten your drawer fronts to the ends of all the drawer side (Q) using glue and brad nails. The top edges of the sides should be flush with the top edges of the drawer fronts. The rabbets on the bottom of the drawer fronts should extend past the drawer sides **(Figure 16)**.

STEP 17: Install the drawer bottoms (S). They fit in the rabbets at the bottom of the drawer fronts **(Figure 18)**, but they are not long enough to extend the entire length of the drawer sides. This is done intentionally so the drawers can slide out far enough so that you can see all the way to the back without their falling out of the cabinet.

STEP 18: Finally, install the drawer backs (R) between the drawer sides and at the back edge of the drawer bottoms **(Figure 19)**.

Need a Lift?

While this table was designed to fit my homemade router lift, you may also install your own commercial lift (or no lift at all). Just keep in mind that whatever lift you use must fit in the 10¾" wide space between the two drawer banks.

Stumpy Nubs Woodworking
PRO TIP

Figure 16

Figure 17

Figure 18

Figure 19

PART FOUR: MOUNTING THE ROUTER PLATE

STEP 19: Whether you are mounting your own router plate or my homemade router lift, you will begin by placing your plate on the top of your table. Be sure it is exactly centered between the two sides, and about 1½" from and parallel to the sliding carriage. When you are satisfied that it's positioned correctly, carefully trace its profile with a sharp pencil (**Figure 20**).

STEP 20: Install a ½" straight bit in a plunge router and set the depth to the thickness of your router plate, plus about ⅟₃₂". Carefully rout around the perimeter of your square, staying about ⅟₁₆" away from the pencil line. Return with a second pass, nibbling away the rest of the material up to the line. In this way you can freehand rout quickly and accurately (**Figure 21**).

STEP 21: Use a jigsaw to cut out the center. Follow the inner edge of the groove your router made. This will create a rabbet all around the opening (**Figure 22**).

Figure 20

Figure 21

Figure 22

STEP 22: Install your router lift or plate. Use paper shims to bring it up flush with the top of the table if needed. The weight of the router and lift, along with the friction fit around the edges, should keep it securely in place **(Figure 23)**.

STEP 23: If you are installing my homemade lift, you will have to remove the front locking knob and push the carriage bolt into the lift as far as it will go. Depending on how long that carriage bolt is, you may have to trim it back with a hacksaw until you are able to slip the lift into the hole without the bolt obstructing it. You can then reinstall the lock knob **(Figure 24)**. You may mount any fence you like on this router table, but I highly recommend you consider building the incremental fence we designed for it. This fence combines with the sliding table to enable you to cut dovetails, finger joints and a lot more. We'll build that fence in Chapter Three, but first, let's make a lift!

Figure 23

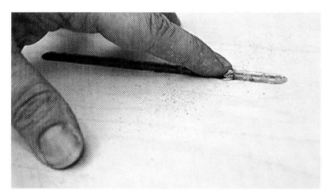

Figure 24

FREE ONLINE EXTRAS

This router table is one the most-used of all the tools we have on episodes of "The Homemade Workshop." These videos will help you get the most out of your project, especially when it comes to using the sliding table feature. We've arranged a series of clips specific to this machine on our website:

stumpynubs.com/homemade-tools.html

Multi-function Router Lift

Router lifts are one of those things that would blow an old-timey woodworker's mind. Actually, routers themselves would probably impress them even more. But the ability to adjust that router far more precisely than by hand, with the lazy pleasure of never having to bend over … well that's the ultimate "how did I ever live without this" kind of tool. Then the old-timer would discover that such a workshop luxury costs about as much as he spent on his best horse and the barn it lives in. Well, let's just say it's no wonder that Thomas Chippendale didn't own a router lift. But as a modern woodworker with a modern workshop full of modern tools, I refuse to lift my own router! So I designed my own router lift.

I'm obviously not the first guy to design a router lift, but my homemade version has a few features that make all the difference to me. For one thing, it tracks smoothly and accurately. But that didn't happen by accident; it took a lot of thought. I used ball-bearing drawer slides for smooth operation, combined with a beveled hardwood track that, when engaged with the turn of a knob, cancels out any unwanted movement that the drawer slides may allow. The router itself is secured to the movable carriage with some custom mounting blocks and a pair of large hose clamps, making it easy to remove and replace as needed. To adjust the lift, you simply turn a nut embedded in the top of the unit with a common socket wrench. The coarse threads on the ¾" lead screw raise the router quickly when desired, while giving you the ability to make the finest of adjustments. The router itself is enclosed in a box, dampening noise and greatly improving lower dust collection by means of a 4" outlet in the rear. The airflow from the dust collector also keeps the motor running cool under heavy use. But the most noteworthy feature of

This homemade router lift also functions as a compact router table. Make accurate adjustments from above the table!

this lift is how it can be used as a standalone unit, a mini-router table with full lift and dust-collection features. You can drop it in the wing of your table saw or into a router table. You can store it on a shelf and set it on the bench when you need it. You can even take it with you for routing on the go, if you're into that kind of thing.

In this chapter I'll walk you through the build, help you select a router, and even give you some tips on making your own router plate. You'll save a few hundred bucks and say goodbye to the old days when you used to lift your router by hand!

Multi-function Router Lift

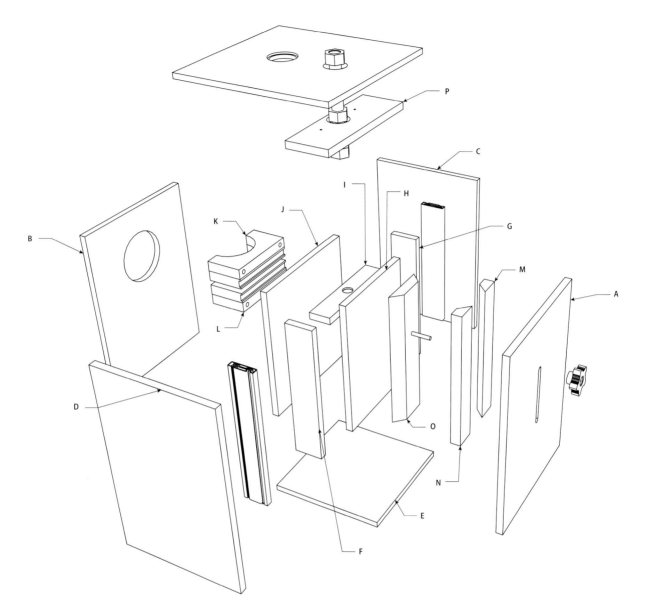

Materials List

QTY	PART	REFERENCE	DIMENSIONS	STOCK
1	Outer box front panel	A	10⅜" x 13¾"	½" plywood
1	Outer box rear panel	B	10⅜" x 13¾"	½" plywood
2	Outer box side panels	C & D	9⅜" x 13¾"	½" plywood
2	Carriage sides	F & G	2⅛" x 10"	½" plywood
1	Outer box bottom panel	E	10⅜" x 10⅜"	½" plywood
1	Carriage panel	H	7⅜" x 10"	½" plywood
1	Lower lead screw block	I	1⅝" x 7⅜"	½" plywood
1	Router mounting panel	J	9¼" x 10"	½" plywood
1	Upper lead screw block	P	3⅜" x 9⅜"	½" plywood
4	Router mounting blocks	K & L	5½" x 2¾"	¾" plywood
2	Outer hardwood tracks	M & N	1½" x 10"	¾" hardwood
1	Inner hardwood track	O	3½" x 9"	¾" hardwood
1	Router plate		11⅜" x 11⅜"	½" acrylic

Additional Hardware

1	¾" threaded rod, 10" long
3	¾" nuts
2	10" long ball-bearing drawer slides
1	¼" carriage bolt, 3" long
1	¼" plastic knob
1	⅛" straight router bit
2	6" steel hose clamps
1	1⅛" socket wrench
	Quick-dry epoxy

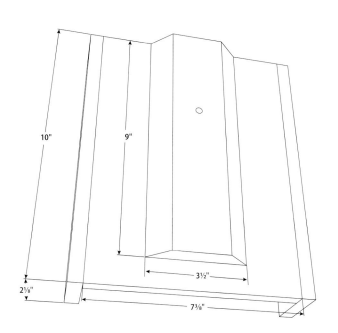

Carriage Assembly

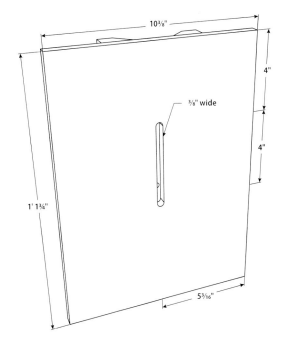

Outer Box Front Panel (A)

³⁄₈" wide

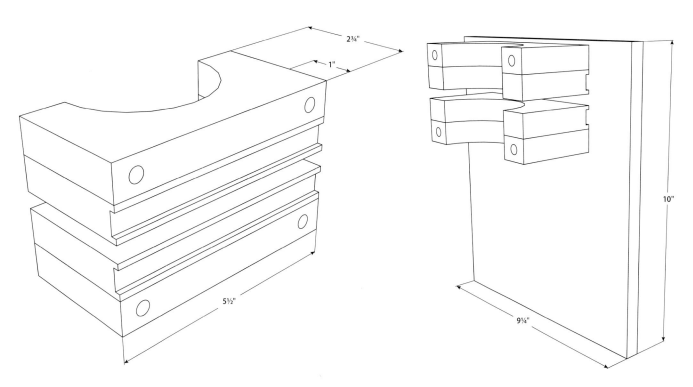

Router Mounting Blocks

Router Mounting Panel

PART ONE: THE CARRIAGE

STEP 1: Draw a pencil line lengthwise down the center of the box front panel (A) **(Figure 1)**. Measuring from one of the short sides, mark across your line at 4" and 8". These points will be the ends of your slot. Drill them out with a ⅜" bit **(Figure 2)**.

STEP 2: You'll have to remove the material between your holes to complete the slot. There are several ways to do it: You can continue to drill holes right on down the line then clean the slot up with a chisel **(Figure 3)**, or you can use a jigsaw or scrollsaw to cut out the waste. When you've finished, set the panel aside.

STEP 3: Find some scraps of ¾"-thick hardwood that are 9" long. The width of the hardwood pieces aren't that important, but the wider they are, the easier they will be to bevel (especially because one piece will have a bevel on two sides). I set my table saw blade to 45° and ripped two pieces about 1½" wide, with a bevel along one edge. I ripped a third piece around 3½" wide, with two beveled edges **(Figure 4)**. If yours are a little undersized, it's no big deal. Just make use of whatever scraps you have. These three parts will make up the wooden track at the front of the lift.

STEP 4: Locate your carriage panel (H). Put some glue on the back of the double-beveled hardwood piece that you just cut and roughly center it on your panel with one end against a short edge. Use a combination square to check both sides of the block, making sure it is perfectly centered on the panel, and parallel to the panel's edges **(Figure 5)**.

STEP 5: Those two carefully joined parts make up the beginnings of your carriage. Now add sides, which are parts F and G on the materials list. Glue them to the panel's edges, pointing away from the beveled block **(Figure 6)**. You can clamp them in place to dry, or speed things up by shooting a few brad nails in them. Then set it aside for a bit.

Check Your Work

As you assemble this project, carefully check the position of the parts. Make sure they are centered if the instructions call for it. Is everything square and parallel? It was designed so that everything will work smoothly if you show proper care as you build it!

Stumpy Nubs Woodworking — PRO TIP

Figure 1

Figure 2

Figure 3

Figure 4

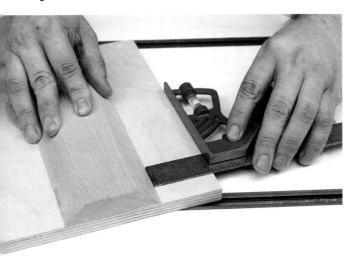

Figure 5

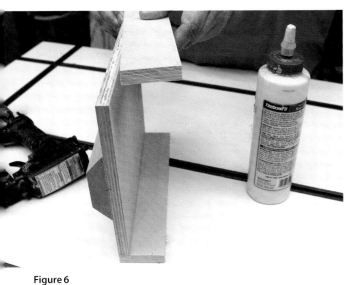

Figure 6

PART TWO: LOWER LEAD SCREW BLOCK

STEP 6: Locate part I and, using your method of choice, find its exact center along its length (**Figure 7**). Now measure ⅞" from one of the long edges and mark where it meets your center line.

STEP 7: Head over to the drill press and chuck up a 1⅛" spade bit. Set your depth stop to bore two thirds of the way through the plywood. (The brad point of the bit can extend farther.) Drill into the center of the piece, then wander around the shop until you locate that drill press chuck key you're always misplacing, and use it to swap over to a ¾" bit. Stick that bit's point in the little hole made by the larger bit's point, and bore the rest of the way through, creating a nice stepped hole (**Figure 8**).

Figure 7

Figure 8

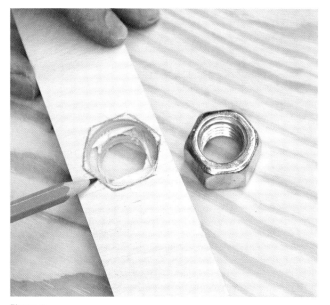

Figure 9

Figure 10

STEP 8: Someday we'll make a jig to drill holes shaped like octagons, but for now we'll just modify this one. Slip your ¾" threaded rod through the hole and tighten a nut on each side of the workpiece, pinching the wood in between. Now, with a pencil, trace around the nut that's covering the larger of the two holes (**Figure 9**). After you remove the hardware, get out a chisel and carefully trim to the line, removing the waste until you have a nice nesting spot for one of the nuts, which you will now epoxy in there, ensuring that it sits flat (**Figure 10**).

STEP 9: While that dries, lay your carriage flat on the bench, beveled block up. Get out your drawer slides and throw away the directions because you probably don't understand any of the five languages they are written in. Separate them into halves and lay the wider portion of one slide next to the carriage with the rubber bumper pointing toward the bottom (**Figure 11**). You don't need a million screws, just three or four per side. It's important that you use a center punch to create a little pilot hole for each screw. You don't want them to wander off center as you drive them home and throw your drawer slide out of alignment. Attach a half drawer slide to each side of the carriage.

Figure 11

They Aren't Just For Sliding Your Drawers

I use ball-bearing drawer slides for all sorts of stuff around the shop. They're smooth, durable and accurate enough to create sliding mechanisms for woodworking jigs. You'll find them in a lot of home centers, cabinet suppliers and woodworking outlets. I like to keep a couple sets of different lengths on hand because I'm always finding new uses for them!

Stumpy Nubs Woodworking
PRO TIP

PART THREE: THE OUTER BOX

STEP 10: Draw a line on panel C that is 2¼" from, and parallel to the right (long) edge **(Figure 12)**. Do the same on the left edge of panel D.

STEP 11: Place the narrow halves of your drawer slides on these lines, positioning the tabbed end against the bottom edges of the panels. Center the lines in the holes and fasten them down with screws **(Figure 13)**. As you do, use a combination square to adjust the slides so that they are parallel with the panel's edge.

STEP 12: Assemble your drawer slides by sliding the carriage between panels C and D **(Figure 14)**, then place your slotted panel (A) on top. Use screws – not glue – to attach this panel so that end of the slot that is closest to the end of the panel is facing in the same direction as the metal tabs on the drawer slides **(Figure 15)**.

STEP 13: With your carriage slid into the highest position **(Figure 15)**, slip a ¼" drill bit into the top end of the slot and drill a hole through the hardwood block and carriage behind it. Later you can slip a carriage bolt through this hole from the inside and secure it with a knob outside the box.

STEP 14: Slip your two single beveled hardwood pieces into the gap between the carriage and the outer box, mating the bevels on the larger block **(Figure 16)**. Slide them together so they just touch. If you pinch the center piece too tightly between them, the resulting track will be too tight. So just touch them together and use a sharp pencil to mark where the corners of the two outer pieces meet the plywood.

STEP 15: Remove the slotted panel and, using screws, mount the beveled pieces in the position that you marked them. Be sure they are parallel to the panel's edge **(Figure 17)**.

Figure 12

Figure 13

Figure 14

Figure 15

Figure 16

Figure 17

PART FOUR:
THE ROUTER MOUNTS

STEP 16: Measure the diameter of your router motor. Now, with some scraps of ¾" plywood or hardwood, lay out two squares as shown in **Figure 20**. The circle in the center is the diameter of your router motor. Cut out the center waste so that you are left with a pair of arched blocks from each square you laid out.

STEP 17: Glue your freshly cut blocks into two little sandwiches. Now, with your table saw blade set about ⅛" high, make several passes starting about ⅛" from the edge of your sandwiched blocks until you have a groove that's the same width as your hose clamps **(Figure 18)**. This groove will be about ½" wide, depending on your clamps, and will run the length of one of the ¾" layers in each sandwich. Place your hose clamp into the groove and bend it to the shape of the block, being careful to ensure that the screw in each clamp will be accessible once the router is mounted inside them.

STEP 18: To attach the blocks to the router mounting panel J, drill holes through the layer of each sandwiched block that doesn't have a groove, one on each end of each sandwich **(Figure 19)**. Drill them oversized to allow for adjustments to be made to the blocks later.

STEP 19: Let's call one of the panels' shorter edges the "top." Place one of the sandwiched blocks about a ½" away from and parallel to the top edge. Place the second as far below that one as the shape of your router motor will allow. Be certain that the blocks are centered on the panel, and parallel to the top edge. Then secure them with long screws, pinching the hose clamps in the grooves beneath them **(Figure 19)**.

Figure 18

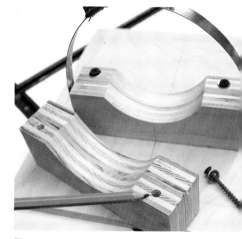

Figure 19

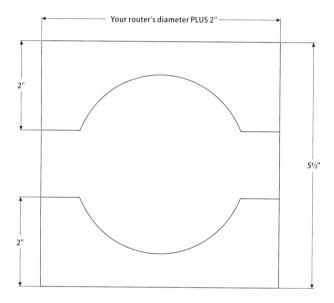

Figure 20

How Much Can You Lift?

If you don't already have a router to mount in your new lift, stop everything and go get one now! There are a lot to choose from, so shop wisely. It's best to buy a fixed-based router because they are less bulky than plunge-based units, easier to mount, and less expensive. A model with a removable cylindrical motor is ideal. If you only plan on using it for light work, you can get by with a ¼" collet model with at least 1.5hp. But if you can get a larger, more powerful router now, you won't have to rebuild your lift to fit the ½" collet, 2¼ hp+ beast you'll need once your skills and projects advance later on. Buy the best you can afford. After all, you're saving money on the lift!

Stumpy Nubs Woodworking
PRO TIP

PART FIVE: LINING UP THE LEAD SCREW

STEP 20: Reassemble the carriage and outer box as shown back in **Figure 15**. With your carriage in that uppermost position, set the lower lead screw block (LLSB) inside its rim **(Figure 21)**. Remember, the nut is off center, so you have to be sure you orient it properly. Place it so that the hole is farthest away from the slotted panel, then measure from the outer edge of that panel to the center of the hole. Be precise, because this measurement is important. Write it down!

STEP 21: Now separate the drawer slides, removing the carriage from the three panels of the outer box assembly. We have to modify the upper lead screw block (ULSB), labeled (P) in the materials list. This has to slip inside the top of the outer box assembly, right over where the carriage was. The problem is the hardwood track and the top of the drawer slides are in the way. So you'll have to hold it in place and mark the spots that will be cut out **(Figure 22)**.

STEP 22: After you've cut it into a funny shape, hold the ULSB back in place and measure from the outside of the slotted panel the same distance you measured to the center of the hole in the LLSB **(Figure 23)**. Be certain that your mark also falls in the exact center along the block's length!

STEP 23: On that spot you'll drill another stepped hold. Begin with a 1¼" spade bit. After drilling two-thirds of the way through, finish up with a ¾" bit **(Figure 24)**.

STEP 24: Now you can attach your LLSB (the one with the epoxied nut) in the carriage. Place it between the carriage sides, about 4" from the top. Remember to position it with the off-center hole farthest away from the front panel on the carriage and with the nut facing down. Use your combination square set to 4" to check both ends so you're sure it's straight before you glue it in place **(Figure 25)**. Some brad nails will strengthen it.

STEP 25: Before you reinstall the carriage, you'll need to insert the carriage bolt into the hole **(Figure 25)**, then attach the router mounting panel using screws. That panel is wider than the carriage, so be sure the overhang is equal on both sides **(Figure 26)**.

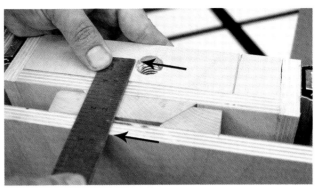
Figure 21

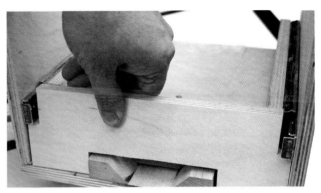
Figure 22

Figure 23

Figure 24

Figure 25

STEP 26: Cut your ¾" rod to about 10" long. Thread a nut on, about an inch past one end. Now apply some epoxy to the end of the rod that's sticking out past the nut. It's OK to gob it on here because when you back the nut up into the epoxy, it will squeeze out the top, which won't be a problem.

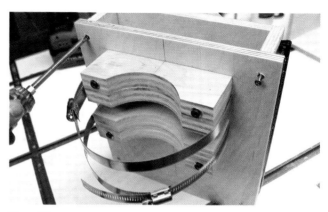
Figure 26

STEP 27: Now slide the rod into the hole on your ULSB (the one without the epoxied nut on it), allowing the nut to rest on the shoulder of the double hole. (See why we didn't want epoxy squeezing out that side of the nut?) Thread another nut onto the other end of the rod until it's an inch or so below the wood. Apply some epoxy to the nut just below the wood, being careful not to overdo it. Once you're satisfied that the threads are covered, hand tighten the nut so that it just touches the wood **(Figure 27)**. Not too tight! The rod should spin freely but not wobble.

STEP 28: When the epoxy is dry insert the end of the rod into the nut in the LLSB, which you mounted on the carriage earlier **(Figure 28)**. Thread it through until your ULSB fits down inside the rim of the outer box. No glue here; use some screws to hold it in place, both in the front and the sides **(Figure 29)**.

Figure 27

What's on Your Plate?

Commercial router plates are usually aluminum, and often expensive. But you can make your own! All you need is a piece of material that's about ½" thick and very stiff. Acrylics are a great option. You can buy ½" clear acrylic from glass sellers. Another option is Corian, the material they make solid-surface counter tops out of. Some retailers sell cutting boards and pot trivets made from the stuff in just the right size. You can also check with countertop dealers and kitchen contractors for scrap pieces. If you decide to go with a commercial plate, you'll have to drill a hole above the top of the lift's lead screw.

Make yourself a cardboard pattern to ensure proper positioning.

Stumpy Nubs Woodworking
PRO TIP

Figure 28

Figure 29

PART SIX: THE ROUTER PLATE

STEP 29: Cut your plate from ½" material, at least 1" larger than the outer dimensions of your router lift so you'll have a minimum of ½" overhang all the way around. Find the exact center of one of the edges and use a square to draw a line right through the center of the plate.

Figure 30

STEP 30: Remember that measurement you wrote down – the one from the outer edge of the box to the center of your lead screw nut? Add ½" to it. Now measure that distance from the edge of your plate, right along that centerline (**Figure 25**). This point should fall right above your lead screw when the plate is mounted, so drill it out with a 1½" spade bit.

STEP 31: Place the router plate onto the top edges of the three outer box panels, centering the hole directly above the top of the lead screw. Be sure the plate is square to the box, not twisted in one direction or the other. Mark four points for screws to pass through the top of the plate and into the top edges of the box. Drill ⅛" pilot holes at those points. Now remove the plate and enlarge the holes in it so that they are larger than the screws. Use a countersink so your screws will be flush with the top, and then reinstall the plate onto the lift with the screws.

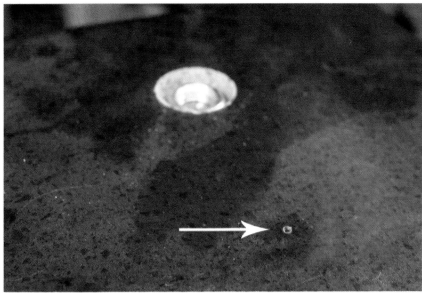

Figure 31

STEP 32: Install a small, ⅛" straight bit in your router, then mount the router in the lift through the open back, securing it with the hose clamps. Turn the router on, and with a 1⅛" socket, slowly turn the lead screw from above the plate, raising the lift as the bit drills into underside of the router plate. Once the bit pokes through the top (**Figure 31**), shut down the router and remove the plate. At the drill press, enlarge that little pilot with your largest bit, at least 1½"-2" then reinstall the plate (**Figure 32**).

Figure 32

PART SEVEN: WRAPPING IT UP

STEP 33: Cut a hole in the outer box back panel (B) even if you don't have a dust collector, because your router will need some airflow to keep cool. The position of the hole isn't important **(Figure 33)**. The size is determined by the diameter of your dust collector's fittings. You should have a nice friction fit when you insert the fitting on the end of your hose. If you use a shop vacuum for dust collection, you should attach it to your fence above the table and leave a 4" hole in the back open. Attach the panel onto the back of the lift with screws, not glue.

STEP 34: Install the outer box's bottom panel using screws **(Figure 34)**. If you'll be using the lift as a benchtop unit, you should add some rubber feet to the bottom, too. But if you're going to be mounting it in our homemade sliding top router table, all you have to do is drop it in! Of course a great table and lift combo isn't complete without a fence, and we've designed just the thing: a micro-adjustable, incremental, lead-screw driven, super-duper joinery fence … which is our next project!

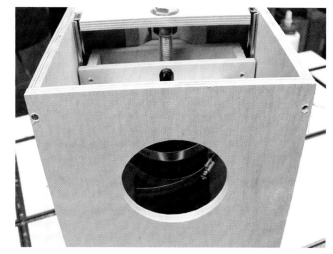

Figure 33

TUNING UP YOUR NEW TOY

Because the router switch is inside the box, you will want to purchase an external switch, perhaps with a variable-speed dial. I suggest slipping a piece of straight steel rod into the router collet (½" or ¼", depending on your router) and using a square on top of the plate to make sure it is perpendicular in all directions. You can adjust the router mounting blocks, or shim under the corners of the router plate to fine tune it. If your hardwood track is too tight, you will have to reposition the two single-beveled blocks, which is why we didn't glue them down. Install a knob onto the carriage bolt protruding from the slot in the front of the lift. This is your locking mechanism to secure the lift during use.

Visit **stumpynubs.com/homemade-tools.html** for video tips on using your new router lift!

Figure 34

Figure 35

Micro-adjustable Router Table Fence

We're only a couple of projects into this book and by now you've likely spotted a pattern. I don't believe in keeping things simple. If you want a run-of-the-mill tool, go to the store and buy it. But if you're going to go to the trouble of building your own tools and jigs, why not go all out? Why not add the features that the commercial manufacturers neglect? This fence design well illustrates my philosophy.

Anything can serve as a router fence – you can clamp a 2x4 to your router table if you like. But a well-designed fence can unlock the true potential of your router, transforming a tool that may be getting little use into one of the work-horses of your woodworking arsenal. This fence is packed with features, and it's designed for accuracy. The secret is the lead-screw mechanism on the base. The standard ⅜"-16 threaded rod provides a positive stop every ¹⁄₁₆". That means

you can set it to one measurement, make a cut, then move it to a different position for another cut, and return to the first position later with absolute repeatability. Turning the lead screw allows you to micro-adjust the fence's position by the tiniest fraction of an inch. And a ball-bearing drawer slide keeps it working smoothly. Plus there's a built-in dust-collection port, and the fence panels that allow you to adjust the opening according to your bit's width!

What really gets me excited about this design is the almost unlimited possibilities. Combine this fence with the sliding top on my homemade router table and you can quickly create tenons, dovetails or finger joints without a special jig. Even decorative joinery that normally requires very expensive equipment is possible because of the positive stops of this lead-screw design. And, believe it or not, this fence is surprisingly easy to build.

A micro-adjustable, incremental router table fence that can turn any router table into a precision joinery machine!

Micro-adjustable Router Table Fence

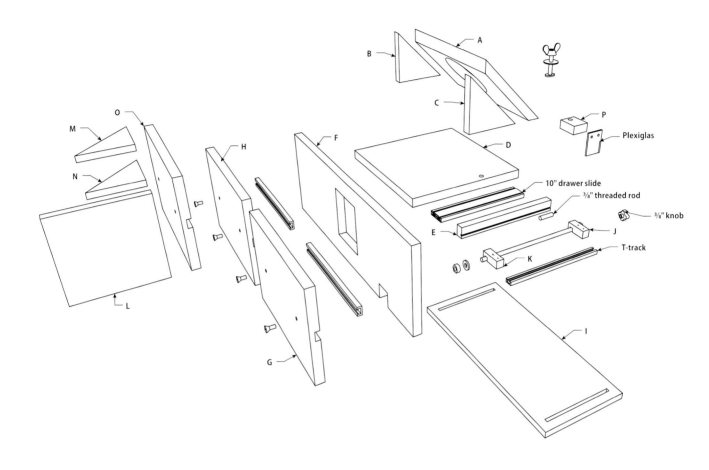

Materials List

QTY	PART	REFERENCE	DIMENSIONS	STOCK
1	Dust cover	A	11" x 8½"	¾" Plywood
1	Dust triangles	B & C*	4" x 4"	¾" Plywood
1	Carriage bottom panel	D	11" x 10½"	¾" Plywood
1	Carriage strip	E	10½" x 1¼"	¾" Plywood
1	Carriage front panel	F	22½" x 7⅞"	¾" Plywood
2	Carriage fence panel	G & H	7⅞" x 11¾"	¾" Plywood
1	Auxiliary fence panel	O	7⅞" x 11¾"	¾" Plywood
1	Base panel	I	23½" x 10½"	¾" Plywood
1	Auxiliary fence panel 2	L	8" x 7⅞"	¾" Plywood
1	Auxiliary fence brackets	M & N*	6" x 6"	¾" Plywood
2	Lead screw mounting blocks	J & K	¾ x 2"	¾" Hardwood

* Draw a line from diagonally across the part and cut to create two triangles.

Additional Hardware

	About 3' of T-track**
6	¼" T-track nuts
1	¼" x 2" T-track bolt
1	¼" wing nuts
6	¼" x ½" flat-head machine screws
1	⅜" threaded rod coupling (or knob)
	About 14" of ⅜" threaded rod
2	⅜" nuts
3	⅜" washers
1	Small scrap of Plexiglas
	Quick-dry epoxy
	Super Glue
1	10" ball bearing drawer slide

**These plans assume your T-track is ⅜" thick and ¾" wide.

PART ONE: THE FENCE

STEP 1: Insert a ¼" straight bit in your router table, and set the fence 1" from the cutter. (If you don't have a fence yet, you may clamp a scrap of wood to the top of the table as a temporary solution). Cut a slot along each end of panel I as shown in **Figure 1**. The ends of the slot should terminate 1" from the edges of the panel.

STEP 2: Draw a small "X" next to one of the slots. Measure 9" from that end. At that point, use a square to draw a line parallel to the right edge of the panel. Now separate the two halves of your drawer slide. Lay the narrow half on your panel so that the line you drew passes through the center of the slide's mounting holes. The end with the bent tab should be touching the edge of the panel closest to you. Use a square to ensure that the slide is perpendicular to the edge before creating pilot holes for your screws with an awl **(Figure 2)**. Pilot holes are very important because a wandering screw can throw the slide out of alignment when you tighten it down.

STEP 3: Cut a piece of T-track 10½" long and attach it to the base panel 15¼" from the end you marked with the "X." Use a square to ensure that the track is perpendicular to the edge of the panel just as you did the drawer slide **(Figure 3)**.

STEP 4: Locate panel "D." Mark one of the shorter edges with an "X" and position it on your bench with the "X" side to your right. Draw a line across the panel just as you did the fence base, except this line should be 2¾" from the edge that you marked with an "X." Lay the other half of your drawer slide on that line. The end without the bent tab should be touching the edge of the panel closest to you **(Figure 4)**. Follow the same steps as before to align and mount the slide.

STEP 5: Attach your carriage bottom panel to the base panel, assembling the drawer slide halves. Lay part E along the edge of the carriage panel near where it overlaps the T-track **(Figure 6)**.

STEP 6: Now carefully cut two of the hardwood blocks as shown in **Figure 5**. These are your lead screw mounting blocks (J and K). Lay the two blocks onto your base panel with the notched ends against the plywood strip, and with a 13" long piece of ⅜" threaded rod in the notches **(Figure 6)**. Now set a 1½" long piece of ⅜" threaded rod in the gap so that it rests on top of the long piece of rod and leans against the plywood strip as shown. With a pencil, mark on the plywood strip where the short bit of rod is making contact.

Figure 1

Figure 2

Figure 3

Figure 4

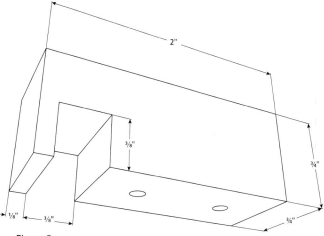

Figure 5

STEP 7: Take the plywood strip (E) to the table saw and cut a ⅛" deep kerf down its length at the location of your mark. This kerf will give the rod piece a place to rest while you attach it with some epoxy, ¾" from the end of the strip (**Figure 7**).

STEP 8: Cut out panel F according to the measurements in **Figure 9**.

STEP 9: Position the base panel (with the still-attached carriage bottom panel) on your bench with the ends you marked with an "X" to your left. Now secure the carriage front panel to the edge of the carriage bottom panel with a single countersunk screw (**Figure 8**). Because the drawer slide is thicker than the T-track, your carriage bottom panel will be tilted at this point. You will have to lift it a bit by hand to get it parallel to the bottom panel, and you will also have to shim under the edge of the front panel with washers about ⅛" thick. This should bring the carriage bottom panel flush with the lower edge of the square cut-out in the front panel (indicated with an arrow in **Figure 8**). Then you can drive your screw.

STEP 10: Locate parts A-C from your cut list. Cut a 45° bevel along one of the 11" edges of part A.

STEP 11: Now lay one of your triangles (B or C) onto part A with one corner aligned with the bevel, as shown in **Figure 10**. Part A was intentionally cut oversized. Mark where the corner of the triangle touches near the end of part A. Cut a 45° bevel at that point so that both 11" long edges of the part are now beveled (**Figure 10**).

Figure 6

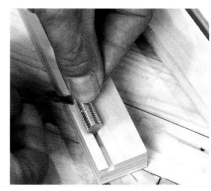
Figure 7

Figure 8

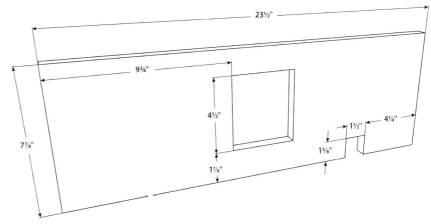
Figure 9

Alignment is Fundamental

Any homemade machine requires a high measure of precision, but this router fence is particularly demanding. Always check your parts for proper alignment before securing them in place. You will be using your combination square a great deal for this one! Pilot holes are also essential because a poorly driven screw will force your part out of alignment. Don't worry; as long as you take your time, you'll be fine!

Figure 10

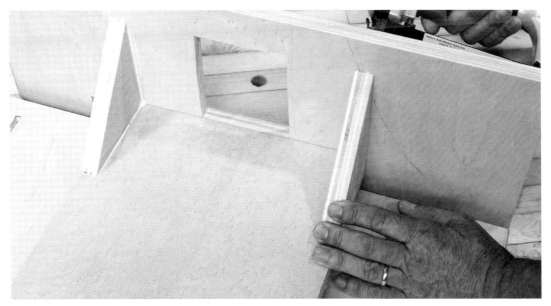

Figure 11

STEP 12: Cut a hole in the center of part A that will fit snugly around the fitting on your dust-collection hose.

STEP 13: Glue the two triangles in place, connecting the carriage front and bottom panels as shown in **Figure 11**.

STEP 14: Part A, with its beveled edges, should fit onto the sloped edges of the triangles. Secure with glue (**Figure 12**).

Figure 12

STEP 15: Secure strip E to the edge of the carriage bottom panel with screws (**Figure 13**). Do not glue it in place; you may have to make adjustments.

STEP 16: Now drill some pilot holes into your lead screw mounting blocks. Screw them in place at the front and back edges of the base panel, with the notched ends touching your plywood strip, and with your 13" length of threaded rod in the notches (**Figure 14**). You should have to lift the edge of the carriage a little bit to slip the threaded rod into place beneath the shorter piece. If you have to lift it so much that the fence front carriage panel's corner hits your benchtop, then remove strip E and reattach it a bit higher. On the other hand, if your two pieces of rod do not mesh at all when the ends of your mounting blocks are touching strip E, then lower the strip, even trimming a bit off its width if needed.

STEP 17: When you are satisfied, epoxy a nut and washer onto each end of threaded rod that faces front carriage panel F (**Figure 15**).

STEP 18: Epoxy another washer and nut to the other end of the rod, tightening it with your fingers only until the washers on both ends touch the mounting blocks. Finally, add a ⅜" threaded rod coupling to serve as a knob on the end, allowing room for your fingers when you attempt to turn it during use (**Figure 16**).

STEP 19: Drill a ⁵⁄₁₆" hole through the carriage bottom panel (D) directly above the T-track. You must remove the carriage to insert a T-track bolt from beneath, then slide its head into the track as you reinstall the carriage. A washer and a wing nut completes the locking mechanism (**Figure 17**).

STEP 20: Cut a ⁷⁄₁₆" deep, ¾" wide groove through the center (lengthwise) of fence panels G - O (**Figure 20**).

STEP 21: Hold one of your fence panels in place against the carriage front panel (F), and carefully mark the location of the grooves (**Figure 18**).

STEP 22: Install T-track at that point on either side of the opening in the carriage front panel (**Figure 19**).

Figure 13

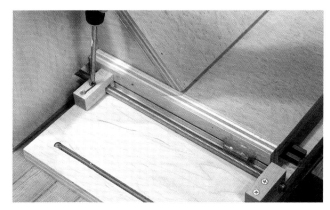

Figure 14

Figure 15

Figure 16

Figure 17

Figure 18

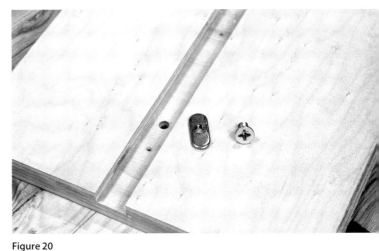

Figure 19

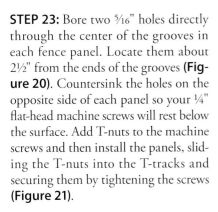

Figure 20

STEP 23: Bore two 5/16" holes directly through the center of the grooves in each fence panel. Locate them about 2½" from the ends of the grooves (**Figure 20**). Countersink the holes on the opposite side of each panel so your ¼" flat-head machine screws will rest below the surface. Add T-nuts to the machine screws and then install the panels, sliding the T-nuts into the T-tracks and securing them by tightening the screws (**Figure 21**).

Figure 21

PART TWO: AUXILIARY FENCE

STEP 24: Position your auxiliary fence back panel (O) on your bench with the grooved side down and the top edge facing away from you. Attach brackets M and N to the lower left corner of the panel as shown in **Figure 22**. The brackets should be about 1½" apart and about 1" from the edge of the panel.

STEP 25: Attach panel L to the bracket assembly as shown in **Figure 23**. Check for square and shim if needed. This auxiliary fence replaces one of your fence panels when you wish to cut special joinery (see Free Online Extras below).

STEP 26: Attach a self-adhesive measuring tape parallel to the lead screw on the carriage bottom panel **(Figure 24)**.

STEP 27: Cut some small pieces of Plexiglas, gluing two together at a right angle to create a cursor that extends over the lead screw and down to the tape **(Figure 24)**.

STEP 28: You may also wish to add a knob to hold while adjusting the fence **(Figure 24)**. This fence is designed to attach to any router table top. You need only drill a pair of holes into your top so that they align with the slots on the fence's base. Use ¼" threaded inserts in the holes so you can secure the fence with machine screws. One hole for each slot is sufficient.

Figure 22

Figure 23

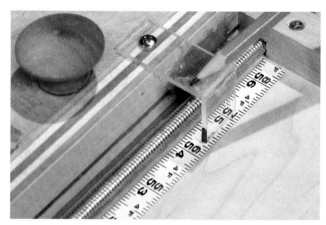
Figure 24

FREE ONLINE EXTRAS

To get the most out of your new router fence, I highly suggest you pair it with our unique sliding top router table. By mounting the fence on the sliding table, you can use the auxiliary fence attachment to create specialized joinery such as dovetails, finger joints and more. We have produced some free video content demonstrating all that this fence is capable of, which you can watch at **stumpynubs.com/homemade-tools.html.**

Benchtop Jigsaw

I've spent a good portion of my time on this earth searching for the answer to one of life's great mysteries: How do they put the hole in a donut? I mean, do they use a drill? Some sort of punch? A coping saw? The research has been delicious, and it has led to creation of one of the most useful tools in my shop. Seriously, though, I'm often looking for a way to remove material from the center of a workpiece. A drill press will work only for relatively small, round holes. A band saw requires entering the cut from the outside edge of the piece, which isn't always an option. A hand held "saber saw" might fit the bill, but it doesn't always fit the workpiece. Larger cuts are no problem, but have you ever tried hanging a small part off the edge of your bench as you try not to rip into your top, or your hand?

What if we mounted the saw upside-down, like a router in a table? You could cut curves and profiles of any shape or size with greater precision and less chance of damaging bench or flesh. It would turn a handy tool into a far handier tool. With the wide assortment of blades available today, you could also cut metal, plastic, PVC and even tile. Now, I will admit that

this isn't an entirely new idea. There is a commercial version on the market. But it suffers from several limitations that I set out to address with my homemade version.

First of all, I wanted the ability to make beveled cuts, and I spent a great deal of time experimenting with tilting carriage designs before I realized that the best mechanism for the job was already built into the saw. (We'll get to that in due course.) Secondly, I wanted a greater capacity than the commercial versions offer, allowing me to cut larger workpieces without hitting the guard post. So I made the saw bigger, and I also made the post removable for virtually unlimited capacity. Finally, as with all my homemade tools, I wanted to build in as many bells and whistles as possible. So I added a roomy storage drawer for extra blades, replaceable inserts for cleaner cuts and better blade tracking, an easily adjustable hold-down for extra safety, and a tilting top design that provides fast access to the saw inside.

This benchtop jigsaw has more uses than you might think. It's one of the most used tools in my shop and I think it will be in yours as well. So let's get started, shall we?

Turn a handheld power tool into a benchtop machine that will become one of the handiest in your workshop!

Benchtop Jigsaw

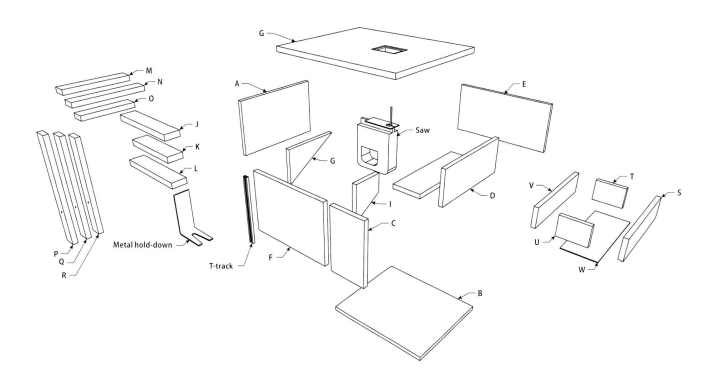

Materials List

QTY	PART	REFERENCE	DIMENSIONS	STOCK
1	Box rear panel	A	10" x 16½"	¾" plywood
1	Box bottom panel	B	18" x 20½"	¾" plywood
1	Box left panel	C	10" x 6"	¾" plywood
1	Box front panel	D	6¼" x 16½"	¾" plywood
1	Box right panel	E	20½" x 10"	¾" plywood
1	Top left panel	F	9¹³⁄₁₆" x 14½"	¾" plywood
1	Top panel	G	18" x 21¼"	¾" plywood
1	Top rear bracket	H	6" x 10"	¾" plywood
1	Top front bracket	I	6" x 5"	¾" plywood
1	Arm layer	J	2" x 10⅛"	¾" plywood
2	Arm layer	K & O	2" x 8"	¾" plywood
1	Arm layer	L	2" x 10"	¾" plywood
1	Arm layer	M	2" x 9½"	¾" plywood
1	Arm layer	N	2" x 10¾"	¾" plywood
1	Arm layer	P	2" x 16¾"	¾" plywood
1	Arm layer	Q	2" x 16"	¾" plywood
1	Arm layer	R	2" x 15¼"	¾" plywood
1	Drawer front	S	3¹¹⁄₁₆" x 16⅜"	¾" plywood
2	Drawer sides	T & U	3⁹⁄₁₆" x 5"	¾" plywood
1	Drawer back	V	3⁹⁄₁₆" x 16⅜"	¾" plywood
1	Drawer bottom	W	6¼" x 16⅜"	⅛" hardboard
10	Zero clearance inserts		3" x 4"	⅛" hardboard

Additional Hardware

	About 9" of T-track
1	¼" x 3" T-track bolt
1	¼" wing nut and washer
	2" x 9¼" thick gauge steel
1	Piano hinge cut to 14" long

Figure 1

Figure 2

PART ONE: THE TOP

STEP 1: Lay out the lines for the rectangular hole in panel G. The rectangle should be 6" from the front edge of the panel, 11¼" from the rear edge, and 7½" from the sides (**Figure 3**).

STEP 2: After penciling in the rectangle, insert a ½" straight router bit into a plunge router and set the depth stop at ⅛". Carefully rout around the inside of your rectangle. Stay about ¹⁄₁₆" inside your line, then make a second pass to remove the rest (**Figure 1**).

STEP 3: Now set your router so that the bit will plunge all the way through the top panel. Cut out the center of the rectangle, leaving about a ½" rabbet (**Figure 2**). Square up the corners with a chisel.

STEP 4: Flip the panel over and align your jigsaw over the hole so that the blade is in its center. Be sure the base of the saw is parallel to the panel's sides. Drill four holes through the base and secure the saw to the top panel with screws (**Figure 4**).

STEP 5: Cut part H from corner to corner, creating a triangle.

STEP 6: Measure 3" up one of the long sides of part "I." From that point draw a diagonal line to one of the corners on the opposite edge. Cut on that line and discard the small triangle scrap.

STEP 7: Attach brackets H and I to panel F. Bracket H is should be ¾" from the edge of panel F. Bracket I is attached flush with the edge of panel F (**Figure 5**).

STEP 8: Attach panels F, H and I to panel G shown in **Figure 5**.

STEP 9: Attach your piano hinge to the edge of panel F on the top assembly (**Figure 6**).

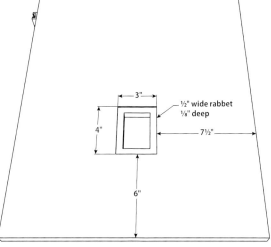

Figure 3

Figure 4

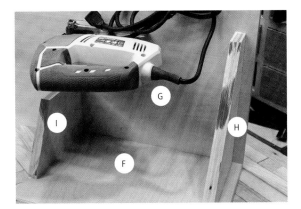

Figure 5

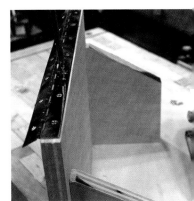

Figure 6

"Jigsaw" or "Saber Saw"?

The heart and soul of our "machine" is a hand-held power tool that goes by many names. The first was simply a sewing machine with a saw blade instead of a needle, an idea which was later marketed as a jigsaw. But scrollsaws were often called by that same name, so many began referring to it as a reciprocating saw. But there was already a different tool that claimed that name. People started calling that tool by its brand, the "Sawzall," until other brands hit the market. Then "Sawzall" reverted to reciprocating saw, and the jigsaw became the "saber saw," which was already another name for the reciprocating saw.

Figure 7

PART TWO: THE BOX

STEP 10: Lay a dust collection hose end fitting near the center of panel A, about 1½" from the bottom edge. Trace around the circumference of the fitting with a pencil and cut the center out with a jig saw. It is best to cut well within the pencil line and then use a spindle sander or rasp to make the hole larger, checking the fit as you do so, until you get a nice friction fit (**Figure 7**).

STEP 11: Next, attach panels A and E to bottom panel B. Panel A will not reach the left edge of panel B (**Figure 8**).

STEP 12: Attach panel C to panel D as shown using glue and brad nails (**Figure 9**).

STEP 13: Finally, flip the C/D panel assembly over and attach it to the A/E/B panel assembly as shown in **Figure 10**.

STEP 14: At this point it would be a good idea to bore a hole through panel A large enough for the end of your saw's cord to pass through. Position it next to the large dust collection hole so it won't interfere with the brackets once the top is attached.

Figure 8

Figure 9

Figure 10

A Good Finish...

If you're like me, you want your homemade tools to look good for a long time. This means applying a finish to shine up all of that nice veneered plywood you used. I prefer a good water based "poly" because it's easy to apply, dries fast, and is very durable. Two or three coats are adequate for most parts, but add a couple extra coats to areas that will experience more wear.

Stumpy Nubs Woodworking
PRO TIP

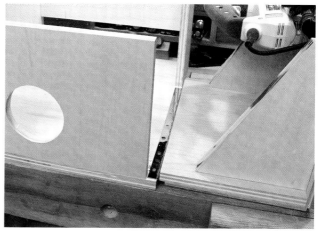
Figure 11

PART THREE:
THE HOLD-DOWN

STEP 15: Cut a 2" x 9¼" rectangle from the thickest steel you can find. Bore a ½" hole 2½" from one of the ends (**Figure 12**).

STEP 16: Use a hack saw to cut from the end to each side of the hole as shown in **Figure 12**. Use a file to remove any burs.

STEP 17: Bend the steel 90° 4¼" from the end you just cut. Then bore two ¼" holes through the other end (**Figure 13**).

NOTE: There are a lot of parts to the arm, all of which have to be laminated together in the proper order to create a stiff assembly. Label all of your parts with their corresponding letters from the cut list and in **Figure 15** before beginning. Always check your parts for square before moving on to the next layer. You may wish to add short headless pin nails to keep each layer from slipping as you add the next on top.

STEP 18: Lay out parts L and O as shown in **Figure 14**.

Figure 12

Figure 13

Figure 14

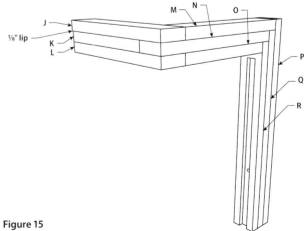

Figure 15

Figure 16

Figure 17

STEP 19: Glue parts K and N on top as shown in **Figure 16**. Be sure the overhang is exactly ¾".

STEP 20: Glue parts J and M on top as shown in **Figure 17**.

STEP 21: Glue parts P, Q and R together as shown in **Figure 18**. Again, be sure the overhang of each part is exactly ¾".

STEP 22: Plow a groove down the center of the assembly that is the same width and slightly deeper than the thickness of your T-track. Stop just short of the stepped area (**Figure 18**).

STEP 23: Mate the stepped portions of the two assemblies together as shown in **Figure 19**. Glue and clamp (**Figure 20**). When it's dry you may wish to drive some brad nails through the joint from each side for extra strength.

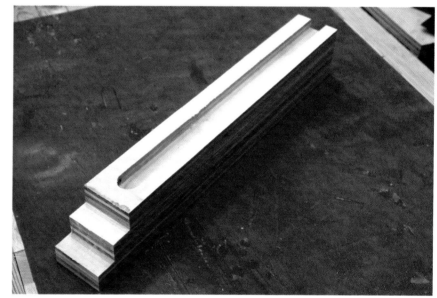

Figure 18

Figure 19

Figure 20

Figure 21

STEP 24: Bore a ⁵⁄₁₆" hole through the center of the groove, 5" from the end. Insert a T-bolt through that hole (**Figure 21**).

STEP 25: Attach a piece of T-track to the rear of the left side of the unit ¾" from, and parallel to the edge. (**Figure 22**).

STEP 26: Finally, slide the arm over the T-track, allowing the head of the T-bolt to slip into the track. Secure the arm in place with a washer and wing nut (**Figure 23**).

Figure 22

Figure 23

PART FOUR: THE DRAWER

STEP 27: Raise your table saw's blade ½" above the table. Set the fence 3⁹⁄₁₆" from the blade and pass part S through the blade, cutting a ⅛"-wide rabbet along one of the long edges. If you have a thin-kerf saw blade you will have to take two passes to remove all of the waste. You can see the completed rabbet at the pencil point in **Figure 24**.

STEP 28: Assemble the four sides of the drawer (panels S, T, U and V) as shown in **Figure 24**.

STEP 29: Attach the hardboard bottom (panel W) so that it sits in the rabbet as shown in **Figure 25**.

STEP 30: You should either bore a finger hole or install a small pull in the center of the drawer front.

STEP 31: Insert the drawer into the saw's box and glue a strip of wood to the bottom panel behind the drawer as a stop **(Figure 26)**.

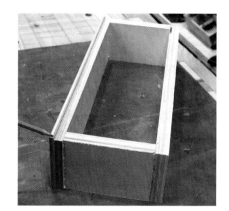

Figure 24

Figure 25

Do Your Drawers Fit?

Because the drawer is small, simple joinery will be adequate. Measure the opening in the front of your assembled unit to be sure no errors have crept in that may require an adjustment to the drawer size. You should also measure the distance from the front of the unit to the front of your saw to make sure the drawer will fit without coming into contact with the jigsaw handle.

Stumpy Nubs Woodworking
PRO TIP

Figure 26

Figure 27

STEP 32: Next, cut a piece of plywood (5⅛" x 16½") to fit above the drawer as a dust shield. Be sure that this shield does not interfere with the wooden bracket (I) when you close the top of the unit. Secure the dust shield in place with brad nails driven from the outside of the box **(Figure 27)**.

STEP 33: The materials list includes several pieces of hardboard to use as replaceable inserts. You'll want them to fit snugly in the saw's mouth opening, so it is better to cut them slightly oversized, sanding the edges down until they fit. To replace an insert, turn on the saw and carefully slide it into the recess, cutting a kerf as you go **(Figure 28)**. If you find that the inserts pop out during use, they are too small for the opening. A solution may be to drive some short flat-head screws through the insert and into the rabbet beneath, countersinking the heads. If you choose this option, be sure to bore the screw holes in all of your inserts in the same place so that they will all align with the same holes in the rabbet. Perhaps, in that case, you should make a couple dozen inserts, drilling the screw holes through the whole stack at once, so you will never have to repeat the process.

Figure 28

Figure 29

Figure 30

FREE ONLINE EXTRAS

If you've watched many episodes of "The Homemade Workshop," you've likely seen all that this simple machine can accomplish. We use it several times a day, and always seem to be finding new uses. To help you get the most out of your new machine, we've posted some tips and other video content which you can watch for free on our website **stumpynubs. com/homemade-tools.html.**

Figure 31

Multi-function Downdraft Table

You know what I hate? Sanding. For me, it's the worst part of any project. I've actually thought about sacrificing a thumb to the table saw just to get out of sanding. Do you know why I hate sanding? Boogers. It seems no matter how much duct tape I use to attach my shop vacuum hose to my sander, I'm still standing in a cloud of nose-clogging dust. What doesn't reach my lungs has to be removed through picking, and it was starting to affect my social life. So I did what I always do: I came up with a solution.

The Multi-function Downdraft Table was designed to solve my sanding problems in more ways than one. It all starts with the interior baffles, which help distribute the suction evenly across the entire top. The top itself is large enough for just about any task, and the ¾" holes provide maximum airflow which will capture the dust before it rises to breathing level. With a good 4" dust collector, this downdraft table is powerful enough for a wide range of tasks that may create fine dust. So we've definitely got the suction down. But I also wanted this unit to serve as a workholding station. So I embedded a grid of T-track which will accommodate a variety of clamps, stops and hold-downs. These not only

secure your workpieces during the sanding process, but give you that extra hand that normally only comes with a traditional cabinetmaker's bench. Whether you're assembling face frames with pocket screws, hand routing edge profiles, or just paring a workpiece with a chisel, the top can hold everything safely and conveniently. I'm not the first person to build a downdraft table. I'm not even the first to embed T-track into a benchtop. But I may be the first to combine the two ideas into one multi-function unit.

Some of the projects in this book are stand-alone jigs and machines. But this is the first of a handful of ideas that are designed to fit into the final and grandest project of them all: The Table Saw Workstation. That doesn't mean that the Multi-function Downdraft Table can't be used independently of the workstation. On the contrary, its compact size and light weight make it ideal for stowing away when not in use. But how you plan on using it will determine the way you attach your dust collector. Don't worry, this chapter will walk you through that, as well as every other detail of the build. Before you know it you'll be saying goodbye to sanding boogers forever!

It's not just for sanding! Keep your work secure and your lungs clear during countless sanding, cutting, routing and assembly tasks!

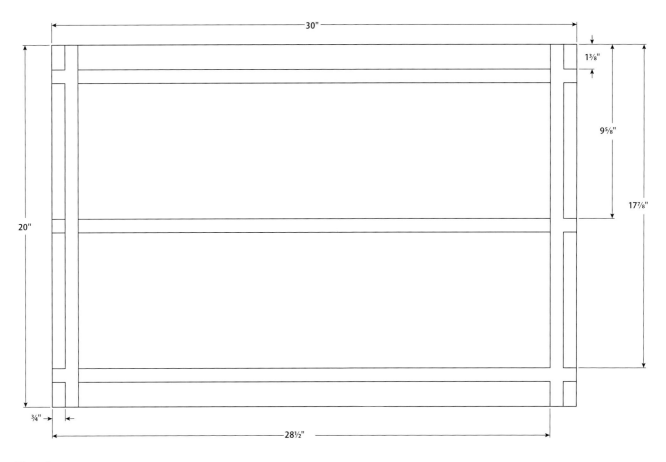

Figure 1

PART ONE (THERE'S REALLY ONLY ONE PART...)

STEP 1: The top panel (A) requires a grid of dados as shown in **Figure 1**. These can be cut with a router table or a table saw with a dado set that is the same width as your T-track. Raise the cutter ⅜" above the table, or equal to the height of your T-track.

STEP 2: Set your fence ¾" from the cutter and run both long edges of panel A against it and through the cutter.

STEP 3: Adjust your fence to 1⅜" from the cutter and run the two short edges against it and through the cutter.

Figure 2

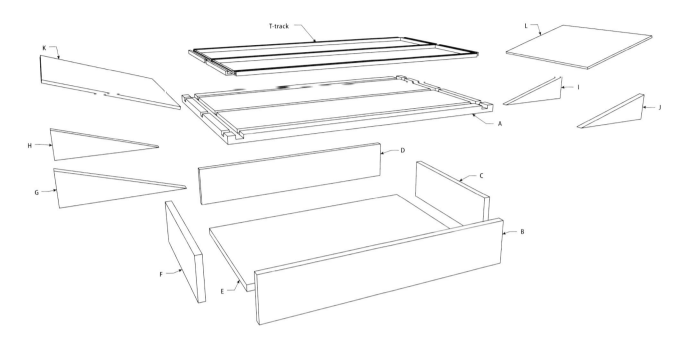

Materials List

QTY	PART	REFERENCE	DIMENSIONS	STOCK
1	Top panel	A	20" x 30"	¾" plywood
2	Front and back panels	B & D	5" x 28¼"	¾" plywood
1	Bottom panel	E	15½" x 26¾"	¾" plywood
2	Side panels	C & F	5" x 15½"	¾" plywood
2	Baffle supports	G-J	3¼" x 10⅞"	¾" plywood
2	Baffle panels	K-L	15½" x 11⅜"	¾" or ⅛" hardboard

Additional Hardware

3   36" lengths of T-track *

1   12" length of T-track *

*The precut length isn't as important as the final sizes. You will need three pieces that are 27" long, and four that are 7½" long.

STEP 4: Move the fence 9⅝" from the cutter and run one of the long edges against the fence again. This should plow a groove right through the middle of the panel, giving you a grid as shown in **Figure 2**.

STEP 5: You may cut your T-track pieces to check their fit, as shown in **Figure 3**, but don't mount them with screws yet. First you should lay out and bore your air holes. Begin by laying a ruler or measuring tape across the panel as shown in **Figure 3**. Place a mark at 3" and then every two inches after that, up until 27". Use a square to draw lines from each point up across the panel.

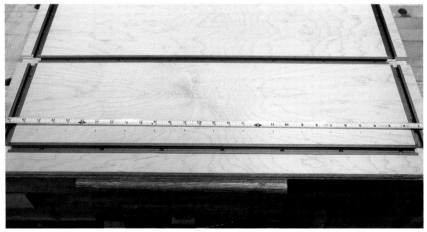

Figure 3

STEP 6: Divide the two large rectangular spaces within the T-track grid into three horizontal rows, boring a ¾" hole along each row at the points you laid out in the previous step **(Figure 4)**. When you've finished, set the panel aside.

STEP 7: Locate your bottom panel (E) from the materials list. If you will be mounting the completed downdraft table in the Table Saw Workstation, you will want to cut a dust collection hole in the center of this panel. In that case, I suggest cutting a hole to fit a 4" blast gate. Position the blast gate in the center of the panel and trace around its circumference with a pencil. Use a saber saw (or better yet, my homemade jigsaw if you've built that project) to cut inside the line **(Figure 5)**. Clean up the cut with a spindle sander or a rasp. If you are using this downdraft table as a stand-alone unit, do not cut the dust-collection hole in the bottom. Instead, cut the hole in the center of the rear panel (D).

Figure 4

Figure 5

Is There a Better Way?

Whenever you create a set of instructions like these, you're bound to find people who want to know why a certain part is designed in a certain way, or why that part is installed before this part … one person's process may differ from another person's. An example is found in the position of the T-tracks in this project. Maybe you want them a little bit farther from the edges, or perhaps you prefer a different grid pattern. But beware, there's almost always a reason behind these design features. In this case, the T-tracks are intentionally positioned above the side panels of the box beneath so you have more material for your screws to bite into. The center track is the only exception. Additionally, the top itself is designed with an overhang so it will be supported by the frame of the Table Saw Workstation, should you choose to combine the two. The moral of the story is this: Sometimes you may have a better way of doing things, and I encourage you to make modifications to these projects to suit your needs. But be certain that the overall integrity of the project won't be compromised before you do!

Stumpy Nubs Woodworking
PRO TIP

Figure 6

Figure 7

STEP 8: Fasten panels D and F to the edges of the bottom panel as shown in **Figure 6**.

STEP 9: Add panels B and C as shown in **Figure 7**, creating a box.

STEP 10: The materials list included two 3¼" x 10⅞" rectangles. You should now cut both rectangles from corner to corner, creating four triangles. These are the baffle brackets (G-J). Glue them inside the four corners of the box along the long sides **(Figure 8)**.

Figure 8

Avoid Tear-out!

I prefer to use a spade bit to bore the holes in the top panel because they feature a longer pilot point than most Forstner bits. I bore the holes most of the way through the material, then flip the panel over to expose the rows of tiny holes where my bit's point penetrated the face. I use those little pilot holes to bore the rest of the material out from that side, eliminating the nasty tear-out common with veneered plywood panels.

Stumpy Nubs Woodworking
PRO TIP

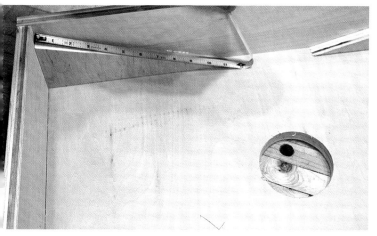

Figure 9

Figure 10

STEP 11: The baffle panels (K and L) are included in the materials list, but I still prefer to measure to be sure they will fit. Measure the length of the brackets' angled side **(Figure 9)**, and the inner width of the box. Cut two panels to fit from whatever thin material you have on hand.

STEP 12: Mount the panels on top of the brackets as shown in **Figure 10**. You may wish to add some caulk to the inner seams of the box at this point as well.

STEP 13: Align the top panel so that the box sides are directly beneath the T-track grooves. Be sure it is square before driving 1¼" screws through the holes in the T-track pieces, down into the top edges of the box. The center T-track requires only ½" screws. All screws should have a flat head **(Figure 11)**.

STEP 14: There are a number of commercially available accessories that will fit your new multi-function downdraft table. My favorites are ¾" posts that fit in the table's holes to support Rockler's Bench Cookies. These are great for holding a workpiece securely above the table, which not only reduces airflow restriction, but protects your top during many cutting and drilling and routing tasks. Many of the clamps and hold-downs available from various manufacturers will also be of great value to you. Of course you may choose to make your own, like a true "homemade woodworker."

Figure 11

Figure 12

FREE ONLINE EXTRAS

This is one tool that you will get a lot of use out of. Whether I'm using a rotary tool, a sander, a saber saw, even a handsaw – anything that creates dust will benefit from this versatile work surface. The clamping options are endless too. You can watch it in action, and perhaps pick up a few pointers on our website.
stumpynubs.com/homemade-tools.html

Shop Vacuum Cyclone

Keep your filters clean and your shop tidy with this shop vacuum modification.

Dust collection is a big issue in the Stumpy Nubs Workshop. It seems that no matter how hard we try to catch it, a layer of dust eventually settles on everything. That can't be good for our insides, can it? Some people pooh-pooh the danger like some sort of coal miner, who puffs out a cloud of dust with every word as he says he doesn't believe in "black lung" stories. I don't know how much sawdust it will take to plug up my wind bags, but I'd prefer to filter it through my shop vacuum rather than my nose hairs. The only problem is those filters plug up too quickly, and the vacuum's efficiency suffers. The solution? A cyclone.

Cyclones used to be reserved for the big, industrial systems found in mills and large production shops. But nowadays they're slapping them on everything from the vacuum you use in your home to the little battery powered gizmo I use to suck crumbs out of my computer's keyboard. Why? Because they work! Cyclones make vacuums more efficient. They take that powerful airstream that's carrying the crud into your vacuum and slow it down, which allows all but the finest particles to drop into the bin before the air exits the cyclone. This keeps the dust out of your filter so you don't lose suction. The idea is so simple that it's almost criminal that shop vacuums don't have cyclones built in. I've been waiting for one to hit the market for years, but like flying cars and light beer worth drinking, the cyclonic shop vacuum has eluded science.

Of course there are a couple of after-market solutions out there, for a price. But we're woodworkers! We make stuff ourselves! So I set out to design an easy to build, homemade version. All it requires is a little bit of plywood, some PVC and a little HVAC sheet metal. You can find everything at your local home center and it won't break the bank. You can attach your mini-cyclone to the top of a 5-gallon pail and strap it to the side of your shop vacuum or, if you aren't afraid to do a little surgery, you can make some major modifications to the vacuum itself like I did. Either way you'll be spending a lot more time cleaning your shop and a lot less time cleaning your filter!

Shop Vacuum Cyclone

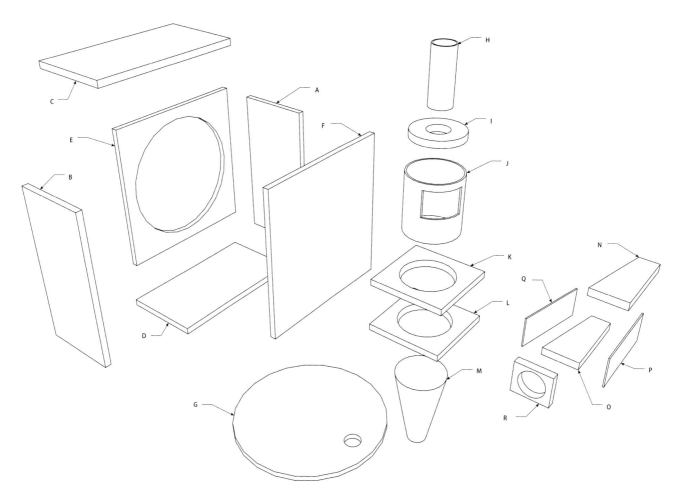

Materials List

QTY	PART	REFERENCE	DIMENSIONS	STOCK
2	Side panels	A & B	19" x 9½"*	¾" Plywood
2	Top and bottom panels	C & D	17½" x 9½"*	¾" Plywood
2	Front and back panels	E & F	19" x 19"	¾" Plywood
1	Dust bin top	G	22" x 22" *	¾" Plywood
1	Cylinder cap	I	6" x 6" *	¾" Plywood
1	Cylinder flange	K	9" x 9"	¾" Plywood
1	Cone flange	L	9" x 9"	¾" Plywood
1	Extra piece for pattern		9" x 9"	¾" Plywood
2	Inlet top and bottom	N & O	3½" x 7¼"	¾" Plywood
1	Inlet end	R	2" x 3½"	¾" Plywood
1	Outer dust panel right	N	21¼" x 2¼"	¾" Plywood
1	Outer dust panel top	M	14¼" x 2¼"	¾" Plywood
1	Inlet right side	P	3" x 8"	⅛" Hardboard
1	Inlet left side	Q	3" x 7½"	⅛" Hardboard

Additional Hardware

	12 x 24" HVAC ductwork-gauge sheet metal
	6½" piece of 6" Schedule 40 PVC or a 6" PVC coupling**
1	2½" shop vacuum wand extension
	3' of extra shop vacuum hose with ends
1	Tube of clear silicone caulk
	Double-sided tape
	Pop rivets and gun
	Screws, glue

* See instructions before cutting to size

** If a coupling is used, you will have to adapt the size of some of your parts because the inner and outer diameter of a coupling is greater than a piece of pipe. Part I will be larger, as will the holes in parts K and L. The upper diameter of your cone will also be a bit larger, and the width of the inlet (parts N, O and R) will be increased.

PART ONE: THE CYCLONE

A piece of 6" PVC (the heavier weight schedule 40, not the thin-wall sewer pipe) is the perfect size for the upper portion of our cyclone. Unfortunately you often have to buy a full 10' of the stuff! If you can't get a 6½" long piece, then you may use a 6" coupling. That will require some of the parts to be a bit larger than they would otherwise have to be, but follow the directions and you will have no problem making the adjustments.

STEP 1: Cut your PVC pipe to about 6½" long (do not cut if you are using a coupling). Center it on a part K and trace its circumference. Cut it carefully to produce a snug fit. Attach the PVC using screws driven from inside the rim. Be sure to drill pilot holes and countersink the heads **(Figure 1)**.

STEP 2: Shop vacuum extensions are tapered, so cut a 6" piece from the larger end **(Figure 2)**.

STEP 3: Cut a plywood disc that fits snugly inside your PVC pipe or coupling **(Figure 3)**.

STEP 4: Set your trimmed extension tube in the center of the disc and trace as before **(Figure 3)**. Cut with your blade inside the line, creating a slightly smaller hole. Since the tube is tapered, it should tighten as you slip it in the hole, cut end first. You want about 1½" of the uncut end to be on one side of the disc when it's tight. Enlarge the hole if needed **(Figure 4)**.

Figure 1

Figure 2

Figure 3

Figure 4

Figure 5

Figure 6

Figure 7

STEP 5: Cut a hole in the center of part R that provides a snug fit for one of your hose end connectors. Use care to keep from making the hole too large and out of round. You want to get a good seal when you slip the hose end in. If you cut in from the edge of the piece, make that cut on the wider side (**Figure 5**).

STEP 6: Temporarily fit disc I into the rim of the PVC cylinder. Measure from the outside edge of the outlet tube to the outside edge of the PVC (**Figure 6**). Transfer this distance to one end of part N. Draw a line from the corner on the opposite end of the part to this point and cut, creating a taper down the its length. Repeat with part O.

Figure 8

STEP 7: Attach part R to the wider ends of parts N and O. You will notice that the cut you may have made from the outer edge to create the hole is positioned on the end of the side piece, which will help you seal it (**Figure 7**).

STEP 8: Finish assembling the inlet by attaching parts P and Q. You will have a gap between the end of part Q and the edge of part O, but you can caulk it later (**Figure 8**).

STEP 9: Prop your cylinder up on the bench as shown in **Figures 9 and 10**. Lay your assembled inlet at the end of the PVC pipe so that the smaller end is centered on the bottom rim. Mark both points on the rim of the PVC as shown.

Figure 9

Sizing Your Circles

There are several holes and one disc in this project that must be sized correctly. A spindle sander or a sanding drum on a drill press will make your job a lot easier. Make your holes a little bit undersized by sawing inside your pencil line, then use the sander to remove the waste up to the line, checking the fit as you go. Do the opposite with the discs. A good fit is especially critical on step #3. If you make a mistake with the other parts you can fix it with some caulk. But step #3 requires a friction fit.

Stumpy Nubs Woodworking

PRO TIP

Figure 10

Figure 11

Figure 12

Figure 13

Figure 14

STEP 10: Set a combination square to 3¾". Use it to draw a line from each point down the side of the cylinder then run your pencil on the end of the ruler to connect the two lines at the bottom. Then reset your combination square to ¾" and use it in the same way to draw a line parallel to the rim of the cylinder, creating a box **(Figures 11 and 12)**.

STEP 11: Cut out the box. The easiest way to do this is with an oscillating multi-tool's plunge-saw attachment, or with a sawing disc attachment on a rotary tool. As a last resort you could bore a small hole in the center of the box to insert a saber saw blade and cut it out that way **(Figure 13)**.

STEP 12: Attach the disc with your outlet tube inside the rim of your cylinder using screws **(Figure 14)**.

STEP 13: Slide the inlet assembly into the opening you cut, positioning it against the outlet tube within. Secure using screws driven through the disc above **(Figure 15)**.

STEP 14: You should have two more 9" x 9" plywood squares left from your materials list. Draw a hole in the exact center of each that matches the inner diameter of your 6" PVC (or coupling if you are using that instead) **(Figure 16)**.

Figure 15

Figure 16

Figure 17

Figure 18

STEP 15: Tilt your band saw table to 11°. (If you don't have a band saw you can use a saber saw, but cut carefully because they are less accurate and blade drift may make it difficult to keep a consistent angle. I suggest either building our home-made jigsaw or our homemade band saw.) Carefully cut out one of the circles, keeping your saw kerf on the inside of the line. The bevel should slope downhill toward the center of the circle. Discard the center, the square is part L.

STEP 16: Repeat the process with your other square of plywood, this time cutting with the kerf on the outside of the line. You will be keeping the circle portion to use as a pattern. The reason you had to do this twice rather than using both the circle and the square portions from the last step is because the saw kerf would have altered the diameter of your parts.

Figure 19

STEP 17: You will need a piece of paper that's around 16" x 20" in size. You can tape four sheets of notebook paper together as well. Wrap a piece of double-sided tape around the rim of your beveled disc from the last step. Place the disc near one of the corners of your paper and carefully roll it across the surface, wrapping the paper around the disc while maintaining the bevel angle. This may take a couple of tries but be patient. The goal is to create a cone that isn't lopsided (**Figures 17-19**).

STEP 18: Once you are sure your cone is properly shaped and that the slope follows the angle on the edges of your disc, tape the seam down its length. Now carefully cut the waste from the top with a very sharp utility knife blade (**Figures 19 and 20**).

Figure 20

STEP 19: Use a measuring tape to mark 10" from the disc down the side of the cone. Do this at as many points as possible all the way around the cone, then carefully cut along the line with your utility knife to trim the cone to length (**Figures 21 and 22**).

Figure 21

Figure 22

Figure 23

Figure 24

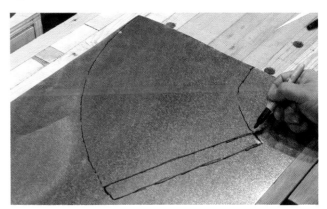

Figure 25

STEP 20: Slit the side of the cone with a pair of scissors so you can unroll it flat on the bench **(Figure 23)**.

STEP 21: Lay your new paper pattern onto your sheet metal. Trace the shape with a permanent marker **(Figure 24)**.

STEP 22: Add a 1" tab along one edge as shown in **Figure 25**.

STEP 23: Cut along the lines. Begin rolling the sheet metal, working it with your fingers. Do not try to roll it into a cone all at once; take your time to bend it a little bit at a time so you won't kink it, especially near the point **(Figure 26)**.

STEP 24: As the metal begins to curl, slip it through the hole in part "L." Slide the pointed end in first, and then work the plywood toward the opposite end as you continue to bend the metal. Take your time and remember you will have to overlap the two edges 1" to achieve the final shape **(Figure 27)**.

Figure 26

Figure 27

Figure 28

Figure 29

STEP 25: You may find it helpful to retrieve the disc you cut out of the center of part L and cut a hole in it. You can slip this over the point of your cone to further help you shape it. Sliding this down the cone will cause it to roll tighter and will prevent it from coming apart as you work (**Figure 28**).

STEP 26: Note the direction of the overlap in **Figure 30**. This is important for proper airflow. Once your cone is shaped, tape the point to hold it together. Secure part L to the top using short brad nails either driven by air or by hand (**Figure 29**).

STEP 27: Secure the seam using pop rivets (**Figure 30**).

STEP 28: Attach the two halves of the cyclone together using screws driven through the plywood flanges as shown in **Figure 31**.

STEP 29: Caulk all of the seams, including around the inlet, the outlet tube, the flanges – everywhere two parts meet.

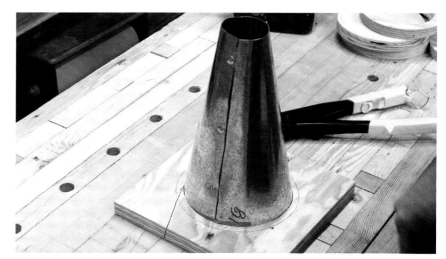
Figure 30

Figure 31

PART TWO: SHOP VACUUM MODIFICATIONS

You may choose to attach your cyclone to the top of a lidded 5-gallon pail, add some wheels and roll it around next to your shop vacuum. But if you aren't afraid to make some irreversible modifications to your vacuum, you can take this project a step farther, creating a more compact unit that holds more dust than a typical pail will.

STEP 30: Every vacuum model is different, so you will have to examine yours to determine how to proceed. The goal is to separate the rim and its latches from the rest of the top. This may be as simple as cutting around the outside **(Figure 32 and 33)**. Be sure to leave enough of a lip around the rim to make it possible to attach a plywood disc as shown in **Figure 34**.

STEP 31: After your rim is removed, cut a disc from ¾" plywood to fit. The rim is attached by driving screws through the channel that slips over the vacuum's dust bin. You may have to countersink the heads or the rim may not fit tightly when you reattach it to the bin. Be sure that your plywood disc doesn't interfere with your latches and that the latches do not stick up above the surface of the plywood or they will hit the upper box once it is assembled and attached. This may require removing some of the material from the latches themselves. Caulk your seams **(Figure 34)**.

STEP 32: Before cutting parts A-D from your materials list to size, measure the distance your filter protrudes from the vacuum's top portion. You want to be sure that your box will be deep enough **(Figure 35)**.

Figure 32

Figure 33

Figure 34

Figure 35

Figure 36

Figure 37

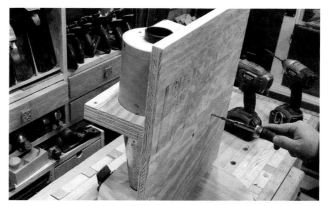

Figure 38

STEP 33: Stand panel F on its edge with the cyclone against it as shown in **Figure 36**. Position the bottom of the cyclone about 4" from the edge of the plywood disc and trace around the point with a pencil.

STEP 34: Use a hole saw to cut an opening about ½" larger than the cone's base at the point you marked on the disc **(Figure 37)**.

STEP 35: Insert the cone's base into the hole and attach panel F to the cyclone using screws driven through the panel and into the wooden flanges. Be sure both the cyclone and the panel are standing up straight before securing. You may then remove them from the disc and set them aside **(Figure 38)**.

STEP 36: Cut a hole in the center of panel E that is large enough to allow the inner portion of the motor housing to pass through while the top of the vacuum will not **(Figure 39)**.

STEP 37: Assemble panels A-E into a box using screws and no glue **(Figure 39)**.

STEP 38: Set the top of the vacuum into the hole and fasten with long screws driven through the housing **(Figure 40)**.

Figure 39

Figure 40

Figure 41

Figure 42

STEP 39: Caulk around the vacuum top (**Figure 41**).

STEP 40: Reset the cyclone and attached panel F in place on the plywood disc. Place your box on the disc and secure it to panel F with screws. Also drive screws through the underside of the disc and into the bottom of the box (**Figure 42**).

STEP 41: Attach the entire assembly to the shop vacuum's dust bin base. Cut a hole in the top of your box to fit your hose end just as you did in step #5 (**Figure 43**).

STEP 42: Caulk all of the seams in the box, except those around panel E, which holds the vacuum's top. You will have to remove this panel to access your filter. Be sure to also caulk around the base of the cyclone cone (**Figure 44**).

STEP 43: Connect the box and the cyclone with a short piece of hose (**Figure 45**).

Figure 43

Figure 44

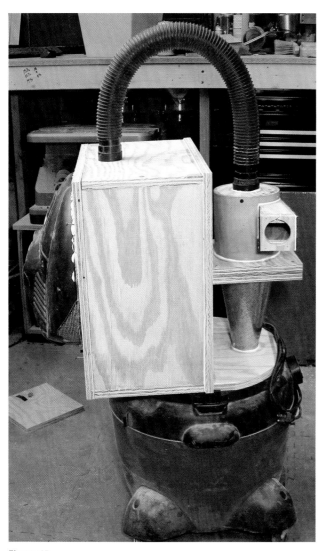

Figure 45

TROUBLESHOOTING

If your new vacuum upgrades seem to sap your suction, there're a few things you should check:

- Be sure all of your seams are sealed. You may even attach some weather-strip between the panel that your motor is attached to and the box.

- Make sure you aren't using too much hose, as this adds resistance. Keep the hose connecting the cyclone to the box as short as possible while still allowing for a smooth bend. And do not use more than about 8' of hose to attach your wand.

- Check your filter for clogs. If fine dust is still causing a problem, consider adding a bag filter that slips over your main filter.

- Depending on the shape of your vacuum's base, the modifications may make it top heavy. If it tips easily you might attach a wider plywood base to the entire unit.

Visit **stumpynubs.com/homemadetools.html** to watch a bonus video about building and using your new cyclone!

Crosscut 'Super-Sled'

I once made a wooden toy for a child. It was a simple little truck that I'd carved to shape with a band saw and slapped some wheels on. No big deal, right? Well that child looked up at me and said something that made me very uncomfortable. He said: "Stumpy, you're my hero." Could I accept such a compliment for a hunk of wood shaped like a truck? Not in my shop! I leaned in close to the kids face and said, "I'm no hero, son. The real heroes are the guys who go to work every day, maybe writing stories for a local newspaper. Then they step into telephone booths and change into colorful tights so they can spend their evenings fighting for peace, justice and the American way." (You didn't really think I'd miss a chance to make a "super hero" joke in the "Super-Sled" chapter, did you?)

You've seen crosscut sleds before, so you may wonder what makes this one so "super." I'll bottom line it for you. This sled has it all. It doesn't just crosscut, it's a feature-packed joinery machine. It will help you cut tenons, bridle joints, half-laps, finger/box joints, miters, bevels, splined miters, splined bevels and a whole lot more. And it will do it with a level of accuracy that no other crosscut sled out there can top.

Let's start with the sled itself. I've added a track to the fence to accommodate a moveable stop for making repeated cuts. If your cut is longer than the fence, you simply slide one of the long extension wings out. These also help support your work. If you want to fine-tune your cut you can use one of the micro-adjusters. Your cuts will be cleaner because this sled features replaceable zero-clearance inserts. There are also slots for attaching adjustable miter fences and hold-down clamps for extra precision and safety. Next is the tenon jig, designed to hold a workpiece on end for a wide range of cuts. It attaches right to the sled's fence and is fully adjustable, including a built-in clamp to secure your work. A spline-cutting jig holds your boxes or frames at a 45° angle for decorative joinery that will strengthen your miters. And finally, a fully adjustable finger joint/box joint jig will create virtually any layout. All of the jigs take advantage of the micro-adjusters as well.

This isn't for your quick, everyday crosscuts. It's a workhorse. And once you build yours, you are sure to wonder how you ever got along without it. In fact, you may even call this sled the "super hero" of your workshop. (But you'll have to send me a nickle every time you do for royalties. At least I think that's how it works…).

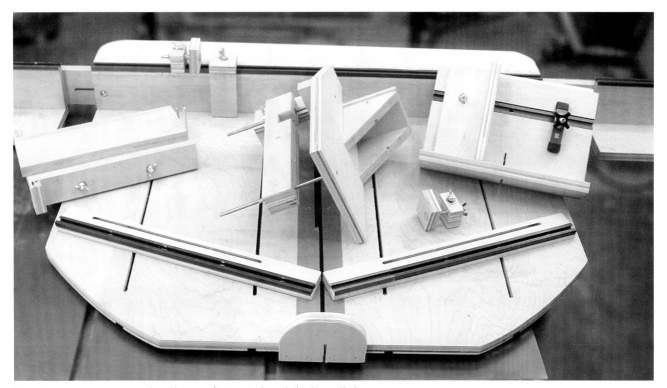

Complete accurate crosscuts and a wide array of joinery tasks with this Super-Sled!

Crosscut "Super-Sled"

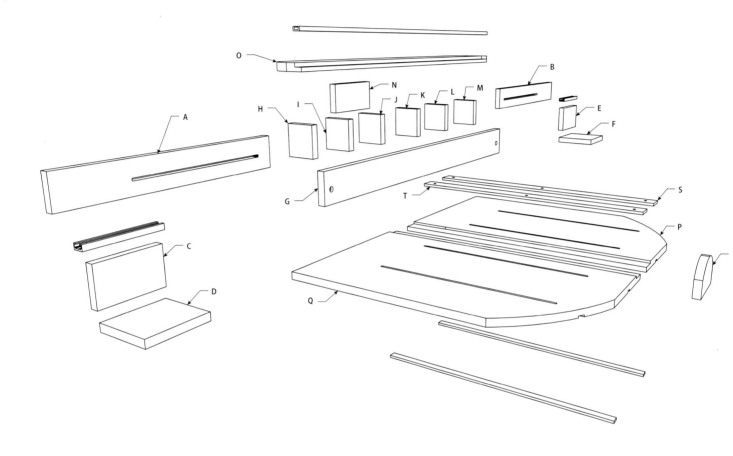

Materials List (Sled Only)

QTY	PART	REFERENCE	DIMENSIONS	STOCK
2	Fence extensions	A & B	3⅛" x 22¾"	¾" plywood
2	Extension spacers	C & E	6" x 3½"	¾" plywood
2	Extension supports	D & F	6" x 5½"	¾" plywood
1	Fence face	G	3" x 36"	¾" plywood
6	Fence bracket blocks	H-M	3⅛" x 3"	¾" plywood
1	Fence guard	N	3⅛" x 6½"	¾" plywood
1	Fence top	O	4½" x 36"	¾" plywood
2	Sled panels	P & Q	18" x 28½"	¾" plywood
1	Sled end connector	R	3¼" x 5"	¾" plywood
2	Miter fences		2" x 18"	¾" plywood
10	Zero-clearance inserts	S & T	1½" x 24"	¼" MDF

Additional Hardware

	Miter slot runner bars*
	48" of T-track
2	¼" X 2½" carriage bolts
4	¼" X 2" T-track bolts
10	¼" wing nuts and washers

*you may also make your own

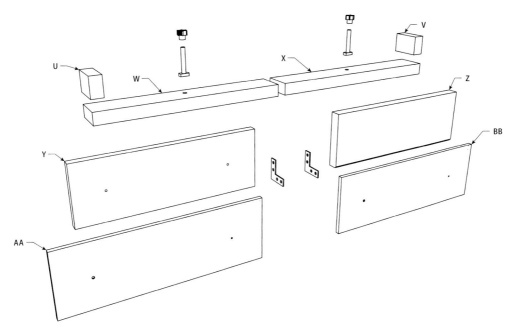

Materials List (Finger Joint Attachment)

QTY	PART	REFERENCE	DIMENSIONS	STOCK
2	Adjuster blocks	U & V	1⅞" x 1¼"	¾" plywood
2	Fence tops	W & X	1⅞" x 12"	¾" plywood
2	Fence panels	Y & Z	3⅞" x 12"	¾" plywood
10	Sacrificial panels	AA & BB	4" x 12"	¼" MDF

Additional Hardware

12" of T-track
1   ¼" x 1½ T-track bolts
1   ¼" wing nuts and washers

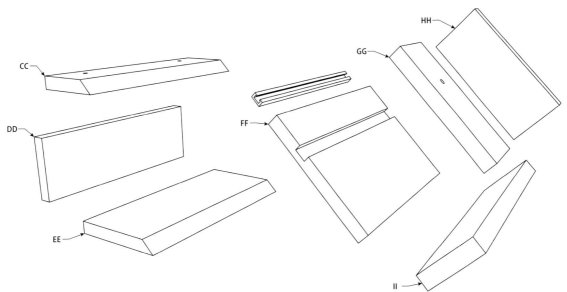

Materials List (Spline Cutter Attachment)

QTY	PART	REFERENCE	DIMENSIONS	STOCK
1	Rear top	CC	12" x 3⅞"	¾" plywood
1	Rear back	DD	12" x 3⅞"	¾" plywood
1	Rear bottom	EE	12" x 5¹¹⁄₁₆"	¾" plywood
1	Box platform	FF	12" x 7⅝"	¾" plywood
1	Fence base	GG	3" x 6⅞"	¾" plywood
1	Fence	HH	3" x 6⅞"	¾" plywood
1	Box platform base	II	12" x 3"	¾" plywood

Additional Hardware

2   ¾ wide, 3 x 3" 90° brackets*
4   ¼" x 2½ T-track bolts
4   ¼" wing nuts and washers

*or whatever size is available

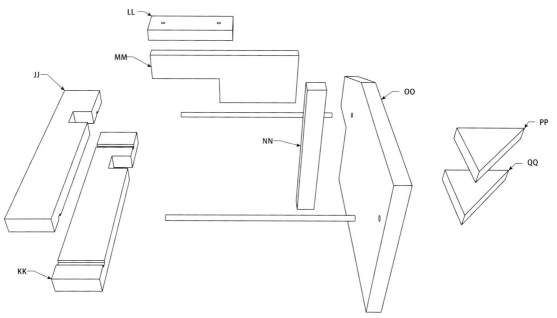

Materials List (Tenon Attachment)

QTY	PART	REFERENCE	DIMENSIONS	STOCK
2	Clamp blocks	JJ & KK	10¼" x 2"	¾" plywood
1	Fence bracket top	LL	6" x 2¼"	¾" plywood
1	Fence bracket face	MM	10¾" x 3⅞"	¾" plywood
1	Alignment stop	NN	1" x 8"	¾" plywood
1	Main panel	OO	12¼" x 8"	¾" plywood
1	Panel supports	PP & QQ	4" x 4"	¾" plywood

Additional Hardware

2	8" long, ¼" threaded rod
2	¼" nuts
2	¼" wing nuts and washers

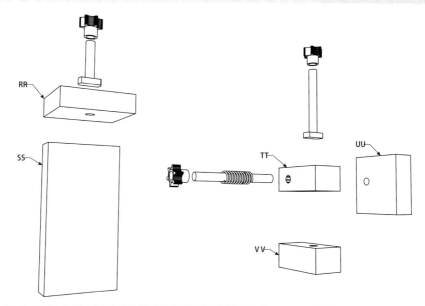

Materials List (Stop Blocks & Micro Adjusters)

QTY	PART	REFERENCE	DIMENSIONS	STOCK
2	Top blocks	RR	2" x 2"	¾" plywood
2	Fence brackets	SS	2" x 3¹⁵⁄₁₆"	¾" plywood
2	Upper adjuster blocks	TT	1" x 1⅞"	¾" plywood
2	Main adjuster blocks	UU	1" x 1⅞"	¾" plywood
2	Lower adjuster blocks	VV	2" x 1⅞"	¾" plywood

Additional Hardware

2	¼" x 1½" T-track bolts
2	¼" x 2½" T-track bolts
6	¼" wing nuts and washers
2	¼" x 3" Carriage bolts
2	Stiff springs ⅜" ID x 1" long
	¼" hardwood dowel

PART ONE: THE SLED

STEP 1: Panels Q and P require some dados which can be cut with a table saw with a ½"-wide dado set or a router table. Raise your cutter ¼" and position your fence 3¾" from it. Run both panels with one of the long edges against the fence.

STEP 2: Now adjust the fence to 5¾" from the cutter. Run both panels again, this time with the opposite long edge against the fence **(Figure 1)**.

STEP 3: Flip your panel over. Using the same cutter height, mill a 1½"-wide rabbet along the long edge from which you cut the first dado (meaning the dado that was 3¾" from the fence) **(Figure 2)**. You will have to do it in several passes.

STEP 4: Position your panels with the rabbets together as shown in **Figure 4**. You will now have to cut the slots shown in that image. They are located directly in the center of the dados beneath **(Figure 3)**, and are stopped 6" from one edge and 4" from the other. These are cut on the router table with a ¼" bit.

STEP 5: Use the same router bit to cut a slot down the center of parts A and B. These slots stop 6" from one end and 1½" from the other end. Position them in the center of each piece **(Figure 5)**.

STEP 6: Use your dado set or router bit to cut a rabbet along one of the long edges of part O to fit your T-track **(Figure 6)**.

STEP 7: If you wish to trim a radius on the corners of your base panels, do so now as shown in **Figure 4**. You may also wish to round off the corners on panel O as shown in **Figure 6**.

Figure 1

Figure 2

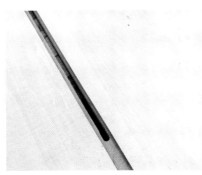
Figure 3

Figure 4

Figure 5

Figure 6

Figure 7

Figure 9

Figure 8

Figure 10

STEP 8: Position the two large panels (P and Q) as shown in **Figure 7**. Blocks H-M are all the same size, so we'll just refer to them as "support blocks." Starting on the left side of the panels, attach a support block 2¾" from the edge, another 8⅜" from the edge, and a third 14" from the edge. Place three more blocks the same distance from the opposite edge. Block N should fit in the center (**Figure 7**).

STEP 9: Attach part R to the far side of the panels using glue and nails (**Figure 8**).

STEP 10: Fence parts G and O can now be attached to one another as shown in **Figure 9**.

STEP 11: Place parts A and B against the support blocks as shown in **Figure 10**. Do not glue them!

STEP 12: Apply glue to the top edges of the support blocks, and to the bottom edge of the fence assembly (parts O and G). Lay the assembly on the blocks and use brad nails driven through part O down into the edges of the blocks beneath, as well as nails driven from beneath the large panels (P and Q) up into the edge of part G. This will attach the fence assembly while still allowing the extenders (A and B) to slide freely between the support blocks and part G. Remove the extenders while the glue dries (**Figure 11**).

STEP 13: While you have them out, attach support blocks D and F to the ends of the extenders. The extenders lie on top of the support blocks (**Figure 12**).

Figure 11

Figure 12

Figure 13

Figure 14

Figure 15

STEP 14: Attach some short lengths of T-track to the top edges of parts C and E, then attach those parts to the extenders, on top of the support blocks (**Figure 13**). Slide the extenders into their slots.

STEP 15: Pull an extender out as far as possible while still keeping the end behind the last support block. Use a ¼" drill bit to bore a hole through the fence in the center of the slot, about 1" from the end of the fence (**Figure 14**). Repeat with the other extender.

STEP 16: You will be slipping carriage bolts through the holes in the fence you just bored, so you'll need to use a spade bit to bore a recess for the bolt head on the other side of the fence (**Figure 15**).

STEP 17: Use carriage bolts, wing nuts and washers to secure the fence extenders in their slots as shown in **Figure 16**.

STEP 18: Stack all of your zero-clearance inserts (T and S) together. Mark a point 1" from each end, centered between the edges. Bore a ⅛" hole through the whole stack at those two points. Lay a pair of inserts into the slots in the sled as shown in **Figure 17**. Extend the pilot holes through the ends of the inserts into the panels beneath. Secure with screws.

STEP 19: Apply double-sided tape to your runners, then insert them into the slots on your table saw. (You may have to place some washers beneath them in the slots to raise them up to the surface level.) Position the sled over the runners so that the blade will cut a kerf right between the inserts. Use your table saw fence to help you keep the sled perpendicular to the front of the saw as you lay it onto the runners (**Figure 18**). Carefully lift the sled off the saw and use screws to attach the runners (**Figure 19**).

Figure 16

Figure 17

Figure 18

Figure 19

PART TWO: TENON ATTACHMENT

STEP 20: There are seven wooden parts to this attachment (see materials list). Begin by cutting the 4" x 4" square into two triangles (PP and QQ) as shown in **Figure 20**.

STEP 21: Lay part OO on your bench with one of the long edges facing you. Cut a 2¼" wide by 3⅞" tall notch in the lower left corner as shown in **Figure 20**.

STEP 22: Measure from the upper left corner 4¼" along the top edge, and 2" along the left edge. Cut from the corner off as shown in **Figure 20**.

STEP 23: Measure 2⅝" down from the top edge and strike a line across the length of part OO. On this line bore a ¼" hole 1" from the right side and 3⅛" from the left side as shown in **Figure 20**.

STEP 24: Lay part MM on your bench as shown in **Figure 20**. Remove a 5" x 2" portion from the lower left corner as shown.

STEP 25: Locate the center along the length of part LL. Bore a pair of 5⁄16" holes along that line, one inch from each end as shown in **Figure 20**.

STEP 26: Glue parts KK and JJ together as shown in **Figure 20**. Cut a notch that is 1" wide and 1" deep in the edge of the parts "sandwich" (which we'll call the clamp block). The notch should be 2⅛" from one end **(Figure 21)**.

STEP 27: Use a drill press to bore a ⅜" hole through the center of the clamp block, 1⅛" from the end closest to the notch. Bore a second hole 1" from the other end **(Figure 21)**.

STEP 28: Assemble the parts (all except the clamp block) as shown in **Figures 22 and 23**. Use glue and brad nails for strength. Be sure to check each part with a square to ensure everything is positioned properly.

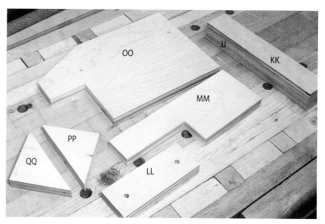

Figure 20

Figure 21

Figure 22

Should You Buy Runners or Make Them?

High-quality aluminum runners for your miter slots are commercially available, and while expensive, they are very accurate. If you prefer to make your own, use a material that isn't affected by your shop's humidity. An old plastic cutting board will do the trick. Carefully cut some strips that are just wide enough to slide smoothly in your miter slots without any side-to-side movement. Use care when screwing them in place as the tapered heads may expand the width of the runners.

Stumpy Nubs Woodworking

PRO TIP

Figure 23

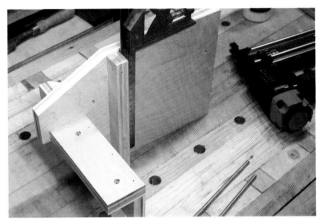

Figure 24

STEP 29: Attach a 1"-wide strip to panel OO just to the right of the missing corner as shown in **Figure 24**.

STEP 30: Spread some epoxy inside the holes in panel OO. Insert your two pieces of threaded rod as shown in **Figure 25**. Attach nuts to the ends of the rods on the other side of the panel, securing them with epoxy as well.

STEP 31: Slide the clamping block onto the threaded rods as shown in **Figure 25**. Use wing nuts and washers to hold it in place.

STEP 32: The jig attaches to the table saw sled with a pair of T-track bolts, wing nuts and washers as shown in **Figure 26**.

Figure 25

FREE ONLINE EXTRAS

This tenon jig attachment can be used for all sorts of joinery, including tenons, half-laps and bridle joints – really, anytime you need to make a cut safely and accurately in the end of a workpiece. For more on how to use the attachment, watch the free videos on our website: **stumpynubs.com/homemade-tools.html**

Figure 26

PART THREE: FINGER JOINT ATTACHMENT

STEP 33: There are eight wooden parts to this attachment (see materials list). Begin by attaching parts U and V to parts W and X as shown in **Figures 27 and 28**.

Figure 27

STEP 34: Strike a line lengthwise along parts W and X that is 1⅛" from what will become the front edges. Remember that the two assemblies shown in **Figure 28** are mirror images of each other! Bore a pair of 5⁄16" holes along the lines as shown.

STEP 35: Attach both assemblies from **Figure 28** to the top edges of panels Y and Z as shown in **Figure 29**. Again, remember that your two assemblies will be mirror images!

STEP 36: Attach your angle brackets to the leading edges of the two assemblies as shown in **Figure 30**. Check to be sure the two brackets are perpendicular to the panels, not bent to one side or the other.

Figure 28

STEP 37: Insert T-track bolts in the holes and secure with washers and wing nuts as shown in **Figure 30**. You will use these to attach the assemblies to the table saw sled's fence **(Figure 31)**.

Figure 29

Using the Finger Joint Attachment

Finger joints (also called box joints) are among the strongest ways to connect two workpieces at a 90° angle. The best part about this attachment is that it is adjustable for various finger sizes. You can also use the micro-adjusters that we will make later to fine-tune the fit of your joint. For more on how to use the attachment, watch the free videos on our website:

stumpynubs.com/homemade-tools.html

Figure 30

Figure 31

Figure 32

Figure 33

Figure 34

Figure 35

STEP 38: Cut a 45° bevel on the edge of parts CC and EE, **(Figure 32)** then attach part DD to part EE as shown in **Figure 33**.

STEP 39: Cut a dado 2" from the edge of panel FF, wide and deep enough to fit your T-track. Use glue and brad nails to secure the edge that is farthest from the dado to the bevel on part EE as shown in **Figure 34**.

STEP 40: Attach part CC behind part FF as shown in **Figure 35**. Drive brad nails through the groove and into the beveled edge of CC, then secure a piece of T-track in the groove.

STEP 41: Attach part II to along the bottom edge of FF as shown in **Figure 36**.

STEP 42: Parts GG and HH make up a sliding fence. Attach them together as shown in **Figure 37**. Bore a ⁵⁄₁₆" hole through part GG directly over the T-track, ensuring that the bottom edge of the fence is touching part II when the hole and track are aligned. This will allow you to secure the fence with a T-track bolt, wing nut and washer, while keeping the fence square.

Figure 36

Figure 37

PART FIVE:
OTHER ACCESSORIES

STEP 43: You will want to make two micro adjusters. They will be mirror images of each other, so keep that in mind as you follow these steps. Begin by gathering the parts shown in **Figure 38**.

STEP 44: Part UU is 1⅞" x 2" Measure 1⅛" up one of the longer sides, and ½" in toward the center. Bore a ¼" hole at that point **(Figure 38)**.

STEP 45: Parts TT and VV also require ¼" holes. Bore them ¹¹⁄₁₆" from one of the shorter ends, centered between the longer edges **(Figure 38)**.

STEP 46: One of those parts (TT) also needs a ¼" hole through its edge, ½" from the opposite end from the one you measured from in the last step **(Figure 38)**.

STEP 47: Repeat all of the above steps to create the parts for the second adjuster.

STEP 48: Assemble the first adjuster as shown in **Figure 39**. Add some glue between blocks TT and VV.

STEP 49: Bore a ¼" hole into the edge of block UU in line with the T-bolt head. Glue a short piece of dowel in the hole as shown in **Figure 40**.

Figure 38

Figure 39

Figure 40

STEP 50: Repeat steps #48 and #49 to assemble your other adjuster, but this time reverse the orientation by threading your bolts through the parts from the opposite direction **(Figure 41)**.

STEP 51: These micro-adjusters attach to the T-track atop the sled's fence. The spring forces the pressure block away from the block, nudging the positions of the various stops and jigs as the wing nut is loosened **(Figure 42)**.

STEP 52: The miter fences require a couple of pieces of 2" x 18" plywood. Hopefully you have some scraps. Cut a rabbet along the edge of each piece that is wide enough and deep enough to fit your T-track **(Figure 43)**.

STEP 53: Use a router table with a ¼" bit to cut a slot down the center of each piece. Stop the slot about 3" short of one end, and 5" short of the other. These two fences are also mirror images of each other, so refer to **Figure 43** for slot positioning.

Figure 41

Figure 42

Figure 43

STEP 54: The fences are secured to the slots in the sled base using T-track bolts, wing nuts and washers. You may attach hold down clamps to the T-track as well **(Figure 44)**.

STEP 55: I suggest making two stops, but one will serve most purposes. The stops are simply two parts: RR attaches to the top of SS. A $\frac{5}{16}$" hole is bored through RR directly over where the T-track will be when it is installed on the sled fence **(Figure 46)**, and it is secured in place with a T-track bolt, a washer and a wing nut.

STEP 56: The stops are wonderful for making repeated cuts. You can also use a micro-adjuster to fine tune its position **(Figure 46)**.

Figure 44

Figure 45

Figure 46

8

Dual-stage Drum Sander

I believe the drum sander was first developed by the aboriginal people of Macca-Lacca-Loco. For a boy to become a man he had to wander into the deep forest in search of the finest plywood tree, fell it with a ceremonial dovetail saw, and construct a machine to sand the tribal drums. If his drum sander worked properly, he could become a warrior. If it failed, he was eaten by a lion. Don't quote me on that.

The modern drum sander is a luxury in most workshops. They are expensive to buy, expensive to use, and expensive to maintain. Yet they are a favorite tool of cabinetmakers because an entire door can be sanded while the craftsman watches with an appropriate non-alcoholic beverage in his hand. That sure beats hand sanding! But I think there should be more to these machines. For example, why should the bottom of the drum do all the work while the top of the drum goofs off all day? Why should we spend a small fortune on replacement sandpaper rolls when the same material is used to make the far less-expensive belts on other sanders? And don't even get me started on the hassles of replacing those rolls! These are some

of the problems I set out to solve with my homemade drum sander, and the result is a machine unlike any on the market.

Let's talk about the "dual-stage" part. I designed the top of the sander to allow access to the top of the drum. This is incredibly useful for fast sanding small parts by hand. You can even use it as an edge jointer for seamless panel glue-ups. Meanwhile, workpieces of any size can be fed beneath the drum for flat sanding or thicknessing. The hand-cranked feed belt allows you to maintain a consistent speed throughout the process. Both the top surface and the lower feed table are micro-adjustable too!

Another innovation that is unique to this machine involves the way you change your sandpaper grits. Rather than buying expensive drum sander rolls, you can use easy to find 6" x 48" sanding belts. And you don't have to peel off one belt to put on another. Instead, you just swap out the entire drum! There's even a place to store your extra sanding drums built right in. Suffice to say, this is the drum sander the commercial manufacturers should have designed but didn't. But who cares, we can build it ourselves! I'll show you how.

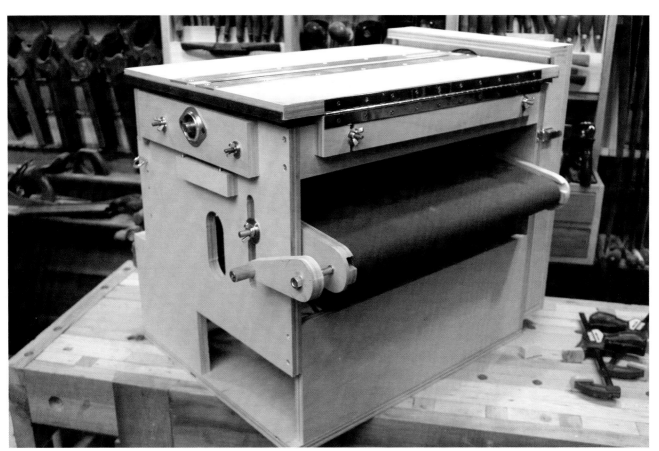

Sand flat parts quickly on the top or feed them beneath the drum – and change grits quickly with this unique design!

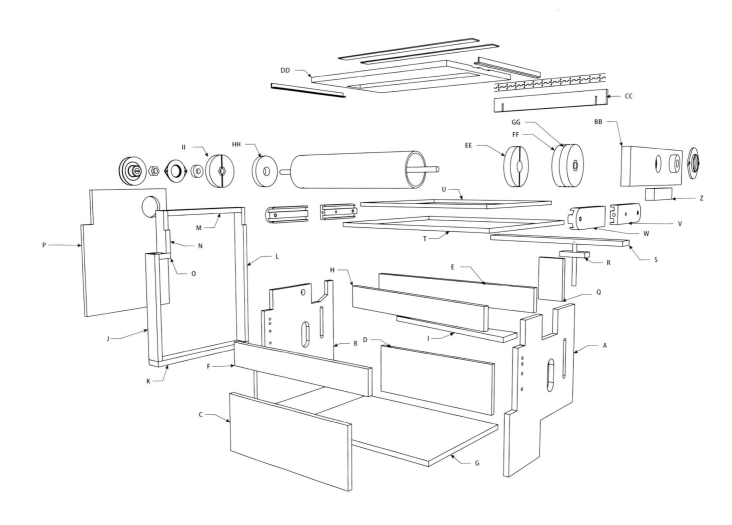

PART ONE: THE OUTER SHELL

This is essentially a box, but creating the complex shape of the side panels will take some work. Lay out your cut lines carefully and double-check everything before you make your cuts. Keeping all of the edges square and the holes precise will really pay.

STEP 1: Lay out side panels A and D according to the diagrams provided. The easiest way to create the large oval hole in the center and the long slot along the edge is to drill a row of holes and then cut away the waste between them (**Figure 2**).

Figure 2

Materials List

QTY	PART	REFERENCE	DIMENSIONS	STOCK
2	Side panels	A & D	19¾" x 19¼"	¾" Plywood
1	Bottom panel	G	19¾" x 26⅝"	¾" Plywood
2	Front & back panels	B & C	8" x 22⅛"	¾" Plywood
1	Left upper rail	F	3¼" x 24⅜"	¾" Plywood
1	Inner angled dust panel	H	2¾" x 22⁷⁄₁₆"	¾" Plywood
1	Inner lower dust panel	I	4¼" x 22⅛"	¾" Plywood
1	Outer dust panel	P	17¾" x 22"	¾" Plywood
1	Outer dust panel bottom	K	17¾" x 2¼"	¾" Plywood
1	Outer dust panel upper left	J	6" x 2¼"	¾" Plywood
1	Outer dust panel lower left	L	15¼" x 2¼"	¾" Plywood
1	Outer dust panel middle left	O	2" x 2¼"	¾" Plywood
1	Outer dust panel right	N	21¼" x 2¼"	¾" Plywood
1	Outer dust panel top	M	14¼" x 2¼"	¾" Plywood
1	Right upper rail	E	2¾" x 22⅛"	¾" Plywood
1	Upper micro adjuster panel	S	2¾" x 22⅛"	¾" Plywood
1	Lower micro adjuster panel	Q	6" x 4"	¾" Plywood
4	Belt table side blocks	V & W	2½" x 10"	¾" Plywood
1	Upper table	DD	24¾" x 18"	¾" Plywood
1	Upper table support	CC	24¾" x 2½"	¾" Plywood
1	Front shaft connector panel	BB	3¼" x 14½"	¾" Plywood
1	Front shaft adjuster block	Z	1" x 5"	¾" Plywood
2	Belt table panels	T & U	19¾" x 21⅛"	½" MDF
9	Drum discs	EE-II	See instructions	¾" Plywood

Additional Hardware

	6" of aluminum T-track
2	24¾" lengths of 2"-wide, ⅛"-thick aluminum flat bar
2	18" lengths of ¾" steel 90° angle stock
1	5" pulley for a ¾" shaft
1	1½" pulley that fits your motor shaft
1	"V" style or link belt
2	¾" ID sealed bearings
2	Surface mount flanges to fit OD of your bearings
5	¾" nuts and a few washers
1	28" length of ¾" threaded rod
3	36" length of ¼" threaded rod
1	12" length of ¼" threaded rod
1	22" length of ¼" threaded rod
1	24" Piano hinge
2	2" x ¾" hinges
4	2" long ¼" hanger bolts
2	3" long ¼" eye bolts
5	¼" wing nuts or small knobs
2	¼" ID X fender washers
2	¼" nuts and a few washers
1	slow speed electric motor, 1-1½ HP
3	20" lengths of 4" schedule 40 PVC pipe
2	20" lengths of 1½" schedule 40 PVC pipe Various screws, wood glue and epoxy
1	48"-long x 20"-wide sanding belt (you can trim a wider belt to fit) Shorter belts will work with some table modifications.
3	48"-long x 6"-wide sanding belts (one each 220, 120, 80)
4	¼"ID x ¾"-long steel spacers

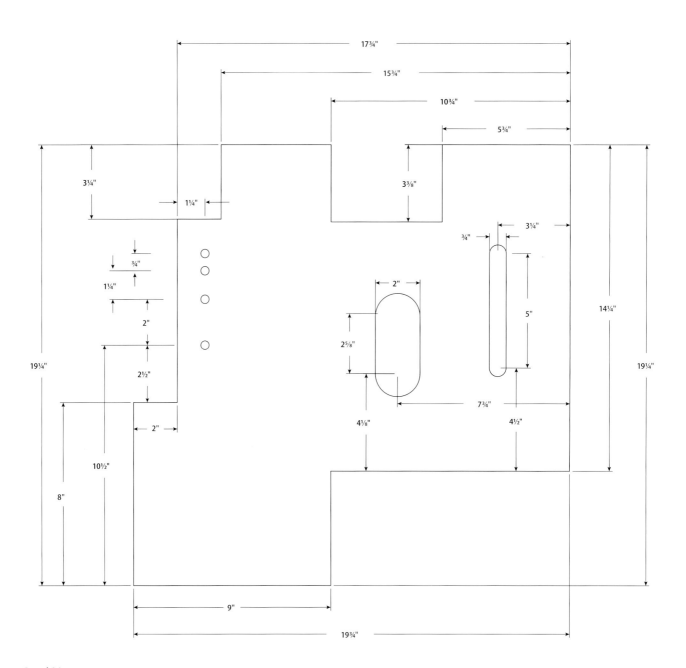

Panel A Layout

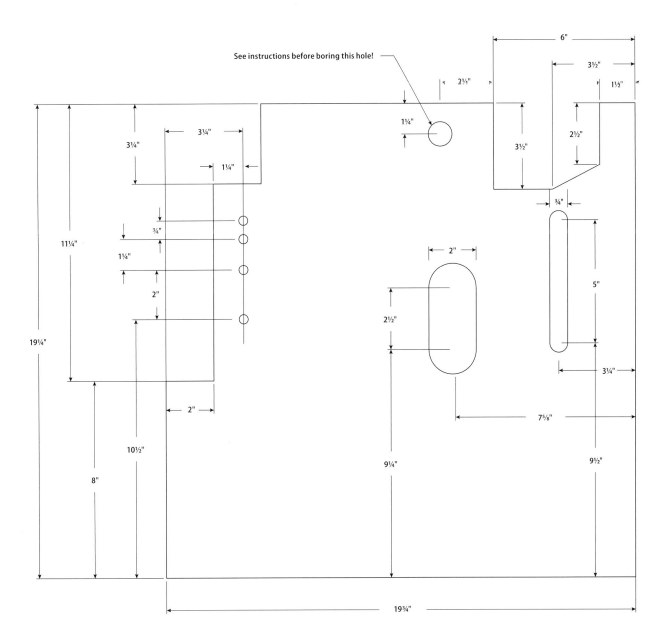

See instructions before boring this hole!

Panel D Layout

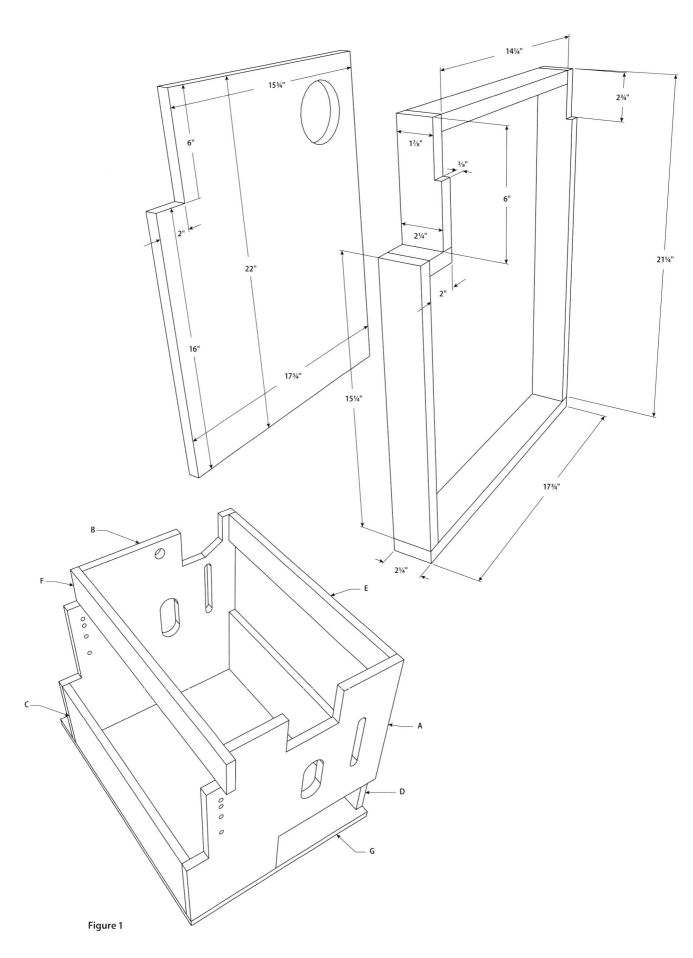

Figure 1

Figure 3

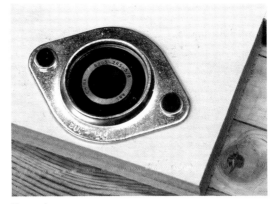

Figure 4

STEP 2: Using a Forstner bit equal to the diameter of your bearing at the point indicated in the drawing, with panel B oriented as shown in **Figure 3**. Bore a little at a time, stopping to set your bearing in the hole and lay your flange on top. If the flange doesn't touch the panel, bore the hole a bit deeper. Be careful not to go too deep or your bearing won't fit properly. You may even create a test hole with a scrap, then set your drill press depth stop before boring the actual panel. (Save the scrap for later.) Once you have the bearing fitted, use a 1¼" bit to bore out the center of the hole **(Figure 3)**. Mount the bearing **(Figure 4)**.

STEP 3: Assemble the outer shell by attaching panels B, C, E, F and G as shown in **Figures 1, 5 and 6**. Use screws without glue. You will notice that panel F protrudes ¾" past the side of panel A. This is intentional. **(Figure 1)**.

STEP 4: To create the bottom of the dust channel, insert panel I as shown in **Figure 7**. Your panel won't be triangular yet, but we'll fix that. Mark where the panel touches the points indicated by the arrows. Then draw a line connecting those two points and cut along that line.

STEP 5: Apply glue to the edge of panel H. Set that glued edge on top of the angled side of panel I. You need not glue the ends of the panel **(Figure 8)**.

Figure 5

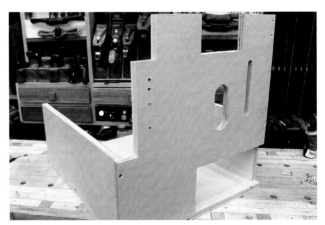

Figure 6

Figure 7

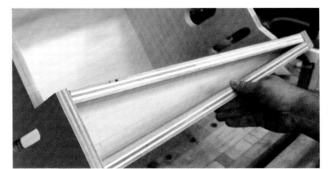

Figure 8

PART TWO: THE TOP

STEP 6: The top panel requires a pair of dados sized to fit your aluminum flat bar. You may use a table saw or a router table. Set the cutter depth to slightly less than the thickness of your channel. Set your fence 6" from your cutter. Make a pass, then rotate the panel 180° and make a second pass. Repeat this process, each time moving your fence closer to your cutter to widen the dados until they are the proper width **(Figure 9)**. Now insert the aluminum flat bar into the dados and check the depth. You want the aluminum to lie perfectly flush with the surface of the panel, so if you need to go deeper, raise your bit and repeat the entire process. It is better to do it two or three times than to cut your dados too deep!

STEP 7: Cut out the center of the panel with a jigsaw, leaving a 1" rabbet all the way around **(Figure 10)**.

Figure 9

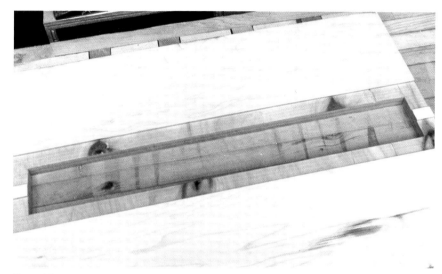

Figure 10

Screws vs. Glue

I prefer to use screws alone to assemble the main parts on this and other machine projects. This allows me to take it apart for modifications of repairs later. I always drill pilot holes first!

Stumpy Nubs Woodworking

PRO TIP

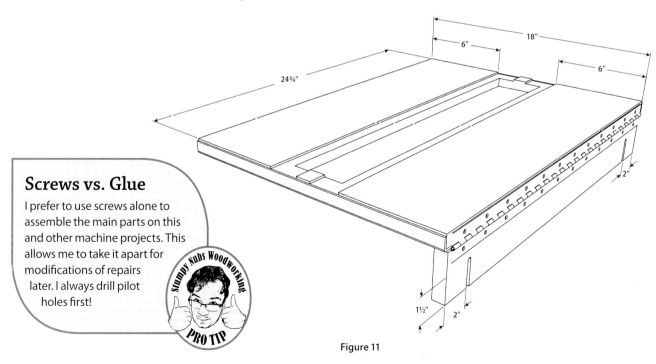

Figure 11

Figure 12

Figure 13

STEP 8: Flip the top panel dado side down and attach steel angle stock along the front and back edges. You will have to drill holes in the channel and smaller pilot holes in the panel. Use four or five screws per side **(Figures 12 and 13)**.

STEP 9: You will have to drill pilot holes to mount the aluminum flat bars as well, but it is also important to countersink these holes so that the screw heads will sit below the surface. Use two screws on each end and five screws along the edge of each piece of flat bar **(Figure 14)**.

STEP 10: Identify part CC from the materials list. Measure 2" from an end, and 1½" from the edge. Where these points meet drill a ⅜" hole, then cut out the waste down to the edge you measured from, creating a slot. Repeat the process on the opposite end.

STEP 11: Lay a piano style hinge along the edge of part CC, folding it 90°, barrel side up over the edge as shown in **Figure 15**. This will ensure that thc hinge is mounted parallel to the edge. Drill your pilot holes but do not insert the screws yet.

STEP 12: Remove the hinge and place it on the edge of your top panel, folding it over the edge in the same way. Drill pilot holes and mount the hinge with screws, then attach part CC to the hinge as well **(Figure 11)**.

Figure 14

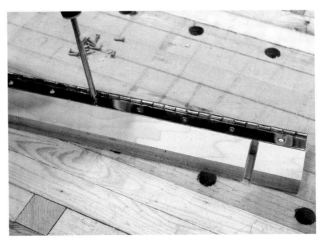

Figure 15

PART THREE: THE FEED TABLE

STEP 13: Locate parts V and W; you should have two of each. Using a compass, draw a 1¼" radius on the end of each part. Cut the curve, then bore a hole at the point where your compass was located. The hole should be sized so that your steel spacers will fit snugly (**Figures 16 and 17**).

STEP 14: Cut dados along both edges of all four parts. They should be ½" deep and positioned ¼" from the edges. The dados should be just a bit wider than the thickness of your ½" MDF (**Figure 16**).

STEP 15: Clamp one of the four parts in a vise with the curved end down. Find the exact center and, using a drill bit depth gauge, bore a ⁵⁄₁₆" hole 2" deep. Take care to bore the hole as straight as possible. Repeat with the other three parts (**Figure 18**).

STEP 16: Place two of your parts side to side. Using a square, draw a line across them that is 3¼" from the curved end (**Figure 19**). Drill ¼" holes on that line, centered between the edges. We will refer to those two as parts V.

STEP 17: Cut out four circles from ¾" plywood. They should fit snugly inside your 1½" PVC pipe. Drill a ¼" hole through the center of each (**Figure 20**).

STEP 18: Lay a ¼" nut on each hole and use a pencil to trace the shape. Chisel out a recess for the nut to set into the surface of the disc. Be sure the nut is centered! Epoxy the nut in place on each of the four discs (**Figure 21**).

Figure 16

Figure 17

Figure 18

Figure 19

Figure 20

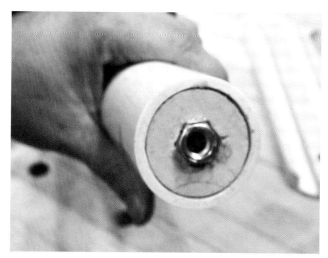

Figure 21

Figure 22

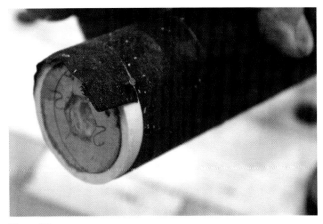

Figure 23

STEP 19: Cut your PVC pipe into two lengths of 20" each. Epoxy a disc into each end, securing it with 1" brad nails driven through the PVC and into the discs **(Figure 22)**.

STEP 20: Cut two pieces of ¼" threaded rod. One should be 22" long, the other 36". You may use a power drill to quickly run the rod through the length of the tubes and out the nut in the opposite end. With the rods extending about 1½" out one end, apply some epoxy to the threads and then back the rod up, pulling the epoxied threads into the nut until the rod sticks out just 1". Apply some more epoxy around the nut on the opposite end **(Figure 22)**.

STEP 21: Wrap the roller with the longer length of threaded rod with friction tape. (A cloth tape found in the electrical department of many stores. Be sure to use the cloth type, not the smooth PVC type.) Fold both ends over to double the thickness and secure with a small nail **(Figure 23)**.

STEP 22: Lay all four of your V and W parts side by side. Using a square, draw a line on the dado face that's 1¾" from the curved ends **(Figure 24)**.

STEP 23: Set both V parts (with the extra hole in them) on their edges with the dado sides facing each other. Apply glue to the lower dados, then slide panel U into the dados and up to the lines you drew **(Figure 25)**. Be sure place the roller with the friction tape between them with the rod passing through the steel spacers. **Figure 26** shows the orientation, with the longer end of the rod passing through the left side.

Figure 24

Figure 25

Figure 26

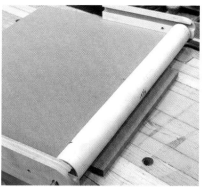

Figure 27

Figure 28

Figure 29

STEP 24: Repeat the process with the panel T and the other two parts, placing your other roller between them (**Figure 27**).

STEP 25: Before the glue dries on your panel assemblies, check everything. The sides should be square to the panels and the rollers should be parallel to the panel edge. Use some brad nails and clamps to secure everything until dry.

STEP 26: Cut two 6" pieces of ¼" threaded rod. Thread a nut onto the center of each piece and slip them into the holes on the ends of parts W as shown in **Figure 28**.

STEP 27: Slide your two table assemblies together, slipping panel U into the dados on the sides of panel T and vise versa. As you do so, slip the other end of the two pieces of threaded rod into the holes on the end of parts V (**Figure 29**). Do not glue!

STEP 28: Trim your belt to fit the width of the conveyor table. Slip the belt onto the table and use a wrench to turn the nuts on each side, extending the length of the table and tightening the belt. If your wrench is too large to fit between the two layers of the table, use a chisel to remove a bit of one of the layers next to where it is glued into its slot as shown by the arrow in **Figure 30**.

STEP 29: Place the assembled table into the outer shell, using ¼" eye bolts as pins at a pivot point on each side. If you are facing the side of the machine with the square cutout on the bottom corner, then the table should be positioned with the long rod pointing toward you on the right (**Figures 31 and 32**).

Figure 30

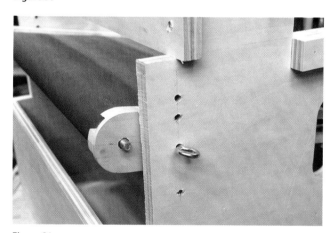

Figure 31

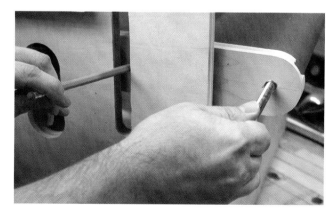

Figure 32

Figure 33

Figure 34

Figure 35

STEP 30: As you tilt the table up and down, find a point on the side that is always visible through the long, narrow slot in the sander's side. Mark that point with a pencil on both sides of the table **(Figure 32)**. Bore a ¼" hole through that point **(Figure 33)**, then slip a ¼" threaded rod through the slot on one side, through the table, and out the slot on the other side. Use large fender washers and wing nuts to secure on both sides of the sander **(Figure 34)**.

STEP 31: Cut a scrap of plywood into the shape of a crank. A good size is 5" long with a 1½" radius on one end and a ½" radius on the other. Bore ¼" holes through the center of each end and chisel out the shape of a ¼" nut. Epoxy a nut in each recess **(Figure 35)**.

STEP 32: Bore a ⁵⁄₁₆" hole through the center of a 2"-long piece of ¾" hardwood dowel. On one end bore a ½" recess, about ⅜" deep. This is to make room for the shoulder of the carriage bolt when you insert it **(Figure 36)**.

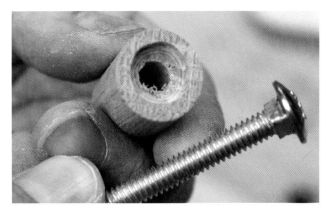

Figure 36

STEP 33: Insert your 3" carriage bolt through the dowel and into the hole on the small end of your crank. The nut should be on the opposite side of the crank as the dowel. Put some epoxy inside the nut and tighten the carriage bolt so that the dowel spins freely **(Figure 37)**.

STEP 34: Thread the crank onto the longer threaded rod that extends from your feed table. Thread it on as close to the machine as you can while still allowing room for the crank to spin without hitting the side panel. Cut off the rod ¼" from the crank, then remove the crank, spread epoxy on the end of the rod, and thread the crank back on. Add a second nut to the stub of the rod and allow it all time to dry **(Figure 37)**.

Figure 37

PART FOUR: THE DRUMS

STEP 35: Cut out nine discs that are just large enough to fit snugly inside your 4" PVC pipe **(Figure 38)**.

STEP 36: Bore a hole in the center of two of the discs that is large enough to fit a ¾" nut inside. Don't go all the way through, just as deep as the nut is thick. Then, with a ¾" bit, bore the rest of the way through. Also bore a ¾" hole all the way through the center of the other seven discs **(Figure 38)**.

STEP 37: Epoxy a ¾" nut in the large hole of your two discs. Be sure to keep the epoxy off the threads **(Figure 39)**.

STEP 38: After the epoxy is dry, thread a short piece of ¾" threaded rod into one of the discs with a nut so that it passes through. Place it on top of one of the discs with the ¾" hole and, using a drill press, bore a pair of ¼" holes through both discs – one on each side as shown in **Figure 40**. Remove the disc without the nut and replace it with another. Bore holes in that new disc as well, using the holes you just made in the top disc as a guide. Repeat with a third disc **(Figure 41)**.

STEP 39: Cut three 20¼" lengths of 4" PVC. Be careful to cut the ends at 90°! (You may use your table saw.) Epoxy one of the discs with three holes into an end of each pipe so that it is flush with the rim. Secure with nails as well **(Figure 42)**.

STEP 40: Epoxy a disc with a single hole (no nut) in the other end of each pipe. Use a gauge of some sort to ensure that the disc sets ½" from the rim all the way around. Add nails to secure **(Figure 43)**.

Figure 38

Figure 39

Figure 40

Figure 41

Figure 42

Figure 43

Figure 44

Figure 45

STEP 41: Cut two 1½" long pieces of ¼" steel rod and file or grind a chamfer onto one end. Insert the non-chamfered end of each piece into the two small holes in the disc with the nut in the center. Secure with epoxy **(Figure 44)**.

STEP 42: Cut a 28"-long piece of ¾" threaded rod. Insert it through the bearing on panel D allowing it to protrude out the back of the sander 2" **(Figure 45)**. Thread a nut onto each side of the bearing, tightening with a pair of wrenches. Next thread the disc with the pins onto the rod. Spread some epoxy on the threads near the nut that's against the bearing, then thread the disc into the epoxy until it hits the nut. If the disc touches the plywood panel before it pinches against the nut, insert a washer between them **(Figure 46)**. (Check this before you epoxy it in place!)

Figure 46

Figure 47

Figure 48

STEP 43: Locate part BB. You will have to bore a stepped hole in this just as you did in step #2, which is why you saved your test scrap. You can use it to reset your drill press depth stop. This hole should be 7¼" from one end and 1¼" from the edge. Mount your bearing as shown in **Figure 47**.

STEP 44: Drive two 1½" wood screws into the end of part BB that you measured 7¼" inches from. Drive two more screws into the long edge of the piece that is farthest from the bearing flange. Position them about 2" on either side of the flange. Allow all three screws to protrude ¼" **(Figure 49)**.

Figure 49

STEP 45: Place part BB over the square cutout on panel A so that it's flush with the top edge and the screws on the end are touching the rail that sticks out on the left. Clamp in place and bore a pair of ³⁄₁₆" holes through both layers, one near each end as shown in **Figure 48**. Remove part BB and enlarge the holes in that part alone to ¾" **(Figure 49)**.

STEP 46: Drive ¼" hanger bolts into the two holes you bored in panel A. You may have to trim the screw thread ends if they stick out the other side of the panel **(Figure 50)**.

STEP 47: Mount part Z beneath the square cutout with glue and brad nails **(Figure 50)**.

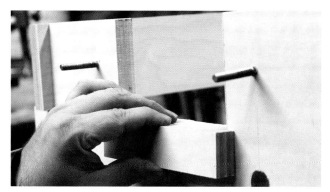

Figure 50

STEP 48: Thread a short piece of ¾" rod through the remaining disc with the nut in the center in the same way that you did in step #35. Use it to align one of the discs with a ¾" hole, gluing them together. Remove the rod when dry **(Figure 51)**.

Figure 51

Figure 52

Figure 53

Figure 54

Figure 55

STEP 49: To attach the sandpaper to a drum, first wrap it without glue to determine the best angle **(Figure 52)**, then mark the material on the end that must be cut off **(Figure 53)**. Spray some high quality adhesive on the first 6"–8" of each end of the paper, then use the trimmed edge as a guide to reproduce your wrapping angle. You need not coat the entire drum in glue.

Figure 56

Figure 57

STEP 50: Slide the drum onto the shaft. The end with the two small holes should mate with the drive disc's two pins **(Figure 54)**. Thread the double-layer disc onto the shaft, slipping it inside the end of the drum as you tighten it down by hand **(Figure 55)**.

STEP 51: Slip the end of the shaft through the bearing on the end cap (part BB), securing it with wing nuts on the hanger bolts. You will need to trim your shaft with a hack saw about an inch from the bearing **(Figure 56)**.

STEP 52: On the other end of the shaft, use a file to wear down the threads creating a flat spot for the pulley's set screw to tighten against **(Figure 57)**. You can then attach your pulley.

Pulleys and Motors

Many electric motors run at around 3,500 rpm, too fast for a drum sander. You should either use a slow speed motor (around 1,700 rpm) or reduce the speed by using a 1½" pulley on the motor shaft, and a 5" pulley on the drum shaft. The motor should be at least 1 hp, although 1½ hp is much better if you plan on using sandpaper coarser than #120 grit.

Stumpy Nubs Woodworking
PRO TIP

PART FIVE: FINAL ASSEMBLY

STEP 53: You will have to use a hole saw to cut an opening for your motor to stick out the back of the sander far enough to align its pulley with the one on the drum shaft (**Figure 58 and 59**).

STEP 54: The conveyor table will also have to be removed so you can access the inside of the sander to mount the motor (**Figure 57**). Set the motor in place and then use some string to measure the length of belt you will need. Wait to secure the motor to until you have the belt in place, tightening it as you screw the motor down to the bottom panel (**Figure 60**).

STEP 55: Choose a convenient place to mount a switch. Feed a wire from the motor, through a hole and to a switch mounted in a gang box outside the sander. Consult someone experienced in safe wiring practices to help you (**Figure 61**).

STEP 56: Assemble the dust panel frame according to the drawing provided (**Figure 62**). Cut a hole in the cover panel that the fitting on the end of your dust collection hose will fit snugly within (**Figure 63**).

STEP 57: Position the dust panel over the back of the sander and mark the position of your hinges on the right side. If you have a piece of piano hinge left, use it, otherwise any other hinge will suffice (**Figure 64**). Attach a latch to the other side (**Figure 65**).

STEP 58: In order to close the dust panel you will have to cut a notch in the frame on both sides to make room for the sander top once it is mounted (**Figure 66**).

Figure 58

Figure 59

Figure 60

Figure 61

Figure 62

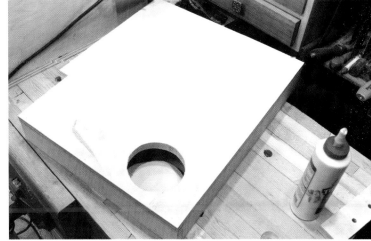

Figure 63

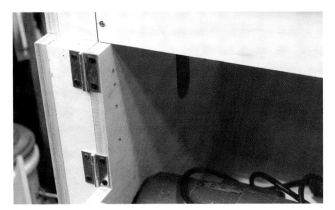

Figure 64

Figure 65

Figure 66

Figure 67

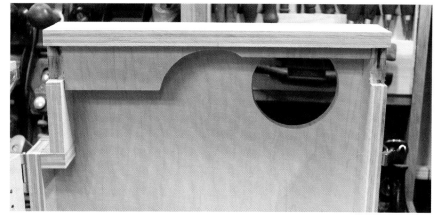

Figure 68

STEP 59: To improve dust collection you may wish to cut some scraps to cover as many of the openings as possible, such as around the top of the pulley. Because this will depend on the size of the pulley and motor, you will have to customize it to your sander. It may help to create a pattern with some cardboard before cutting it from wood **(Figures 67 and 68)**.

STEP 60: Place your upper table on top of the drum. If the drum makes contact with the wood before it does the aluminum flat bars, use a chisel to create a bevel on either side of the opening. This may not be required depending on how far apart you mounted your flat bars **(Figure 69)**.

STEP 61: Locate part Q. You will need to cut a slot down the length of the part, ¾" from one edge. The slot should be wide enough for a piece of T-track to slide smoothly within it. It should be deep enough that the track will be flush with the wood surface **(Figure 70)**.

STEP 62: Cut a pair of 2" x 3" squares of plywood. Bore a ¾" hole through the center of each piece, then chisel out a recess that is the size and shape of a ¾" nut. Make the recess half the thickness of the nut in each piece **(Figure 71)**. Now sandwich the two pieces together with the nut inside.

STEP 63: After your little glue and nut sandwich dries, attach it to Part Q on the opposite side as the slot. Position it against the edge farthest from the slot, and roughly centered along the part's length. Use glue and brad nails driven through the other side of part Q to secure it **(Figure 72)**.

STEP 64: Bore a ⁵⁄₁₆" hole directly through the center of your slot, about ⅔ of the way from the end of part Q **(Figure 72)**.

STEP 65: Attach part S to the bottom of your drive table as shown in **Figure 73**. Use screws only.

Figure 69

Figure 70

Figure 71

Figure 72

Figure 73

STEP 66: Attach a 6"-long piece of T-track to the face of the panel below where you mounted part S (on the sander's outer shell). Position it about 2" left of center with one end touching the panel's top edge (**Figure 74**).

STEP 67: Insert an 8"-long, ¾" carriage bolt in your newly assembled micro-adjust mechanism (**Figure 72**). You can now mount it onto the sander by slipping it over the T-track (**Figure 74**) and using a T-bolt and wing nut to secure it in place. This will allow you to raise and lower the mechanism quickly, then lock it in place. You can then micro adjust the table up and down by turning the end of the carriage bolt.

STEP 68: Set the upper table on top of the sander with the hinged portion hanging over the side that your micro-adjuster is mounted on. The table will teeter on top of the drum, so hold it roughly level while you mark points directly in the center of each mounting slot (**Figure 75**).

Figure 74

Figure 75

Figure 76

STEP 69: Remove the top. Bore ³⁄₁₆" holes at your two marked points and insert ¼" hanger bolts in the same way as you did in step #43 (**Figure 76**).

STEP 70: Replace the top and use a pair of washers and some ¼" wing nuts to secure the table.

STEP 71: Drive a 2" wood screw into the top edge of the sander's side panels just to the left of the sanding drum (when the sander is positioned so that the hinge on the top is to your right). Do so on both ends of the drum. You can drive the screws deeper, or back them out to micro-adjust the table's height in relation to the drum. Large adjustments can be made by loosening the wing nuts and raising or lowering the hinged side of the table (**Figure 77**).

Figure 77

ONLINE EXTRAS

Your sander may look finished, but for it to perform correctly you will have to tune it up and balance the drums. Luckily we've produced a video walking you through the process, which you can watch for free at **stumpynubs.com/homemade-tools.html**

24" Band Saw

This used to be my Mt. Everest. Before I ever built my first jig, I dreamed of one day making a band saw out of wood. I thought about it, talked about it, wrote ballads about it. I changed the names of my children to Band and Saw. I spent years training for this project and when the time finally came, I was ready. I'm proud of all of my homemade tools – except a certain remote controlled handplane that we don't speak of anymore. But this is by far my favorite. While there are more difficult builds out there, the band saw is special. Next to the router, it's the most versatile machine in the shop. A band saw can do much of what a table saw can, while a table saw can't do half of what a band saw is capable of. It can rip, crosscut, re-saw lumber, cut curves and handle the smallest parts safely. It's the unsung hero of the shop, sitting there minding its own business and just plain getting the job done!

I'm not the first to build my own. But most homemade band saws are simply wooden copies of the commercially available versions. As the young folks say, "I'm not down with that." Building any project like this is an opportunity to innovate, to add features that you wish the commercial saws offered. For example, why couldn't a band saw incor-porate a sliding crosscut table like many European table saws have? That would eliminate the need for a miter gauge and open up a lot of possibilities for add-on jigs down the road. And what about capacity? Most band saws limit the size of the workpiece because of a shallow 14" throat. If you want more, you have to buy a giant behemoth of a saw that won't fit inside most shops, or budgets. But a three-wheel design allows us to greatly expand the saw's capacity while actually shrinking its size. And the 10" wheels reduce the stress that typical three-wheel saws put on the blades. Those are just a couple of the design features I added to my saw.

I built this saw with the average woodworker in mind. Few will ever re-saw 12" wide lumber into veneers, so there's no need for a beefy frame that will support the tension a ¾" blade requires. This saw is meant for a ⅜" or narrower blade, perfect for all but the largest res-sawing applications. But where it really shines is in throat capacity. Once you realize the benefits a full 24" affords, you'll wonder how you ever got along with just 14". So strap on your gear and grab the nearest Sherpa, because we're about to conquer this mountain!

A homemade band saw that beats the you-know-what out of many commercial models: 24" of capacity, a sliding table and more!

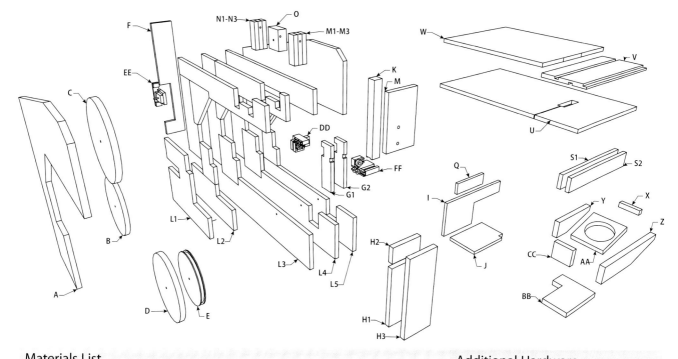

Materials List

QTY	PART	REFERENCE	DIMENSIONS	STOCK
1	Front panel	A	33⅛" x 38½" **	¾" Plywood
1	Wooden pulley	E	9 x 9"	¾" Plywood
1	Left frame panel	F	7" x 27⅜"	¾" Plywood
2	Lower guide supports	G1-G2	3" x 9½"	¾" Plywood
1	Right frame panel	H2	5" x 2½"	¾" Plywood
1	Right frame panel	H1	5" x 9¾"	¾" Plywood
1	Right frame panel	H3	5" x 13"	¾" Plywood
1	Motor side panel	I	8⅞" x 19¾"	¾" Plywood
1	Motor lower panel	J	11½" x 7½"	¾" Plywood
1	Outer guide bar panel	M	2¼" x 8¼"	¾" Plywood
1	Table support	Q	3" x 10"	¾" Plywood
2	Table supports	S1-S2	3" x 19¾"	¾" Plywood
1	Lower table panel	U	20½" x 33¼"	¾" Plywood
1	Upper table panel	W	20½" x 25"	¾" Plywood
1	Sliding table panel	V	20½" x 10"	¾" Plywood
1	Dust assembly back	X	¾" x 3⅛"	¾" Plywood
1	Dust assembly left panel	Y	8" x 2½"	¾" Plywood
1	Dust assembly right panel	Z	12⅞" x 2½"	¾" Plywood
1	Dust assembly front panel	CC	2½" x 2¾"	¾" Plywood
1	Dust assembly attachment panel	AA	4⅞" x 5¹/₁₆"	¾" Plywood
1	Dust assembly lower panel	BB	7¼" x 5⅜"	¾" Plywood
1	Base panel	not shown	38½" x 19¾"	¾" Plywood
1	Upper wheel block	O	3¼" x 3 x 1½" ***	Hardwood
1	Upper guide bar	K	1½" x 1½" x 12" ***	Hardwood
6	Wheel discs	B-D	10¼" x 10¼"	½" MDF

Miscellaneous small hardwood scraps for components DD-FF

*This list doesn't include the parts for the five frame layers (L1-L5). Refer to the di-mensioned drawings for those parts.

** The odd shape of this part means you can also cut several smaller parts from the list using the same piece to save material.

*** You can laminate two or more layers of hardwood together with glue to get the required thickness.

Additional Hardware

4   24" lengths of aluminum T-track

6   Small bearings (salvaged from a flea-market pair of inline roller skates or purchased new)

3   ¾" ID high-quality sealed bearings

3   Flat-mount flanges to fit your bearings (or make your own from hardwood)

3   4" long ¾" bolts

2   ¾" ID steel spacers, 1" long

1   ¾" ID steel spacers, 2" long

1   4"-long ⅜" bolt

    Several ¾" ID washers to use a shims on the wheel shafts.

1   ½-¾HP slow-speed motor (around 1,700 RPM)

1   Link style "V" belt. A standard belt can also be used, but you will have to measure with a piece of string to find the correct size (see step #37). This may require some trial and error, which is why adjustable link belts are preferred.

1   104" band saw blade

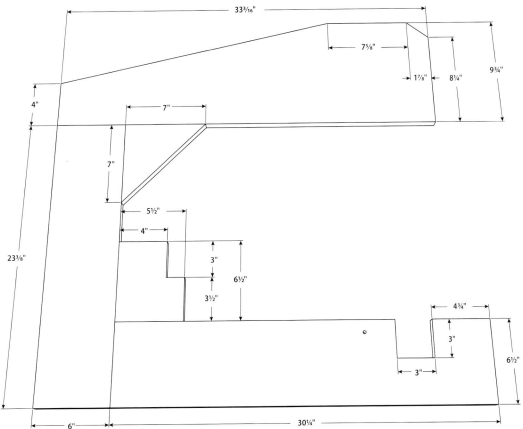

Frame Layer One

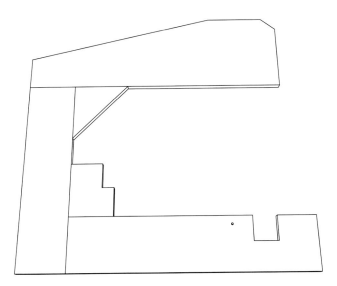

Laminating the Frame

The frame is constructed in layers of components to reduce material waste. These parts are not included on the materials list. Arrange the parts however you like as you lay out your cuts on your plywood sheet. Grain direction won't matter.

¾" cabinet grade plywood is best. Pine plywood is not recommended. Lay out the parts of one layer on a flat surface, then coat them with glue. Also coat the parts of the next layer that will lie upon it. Use brad nails or screws to attach each layer to the one below it so the parts won't slip out of place while you are positioning the next layer. Take care to position each layer properly, checking for square before moving on to the next.

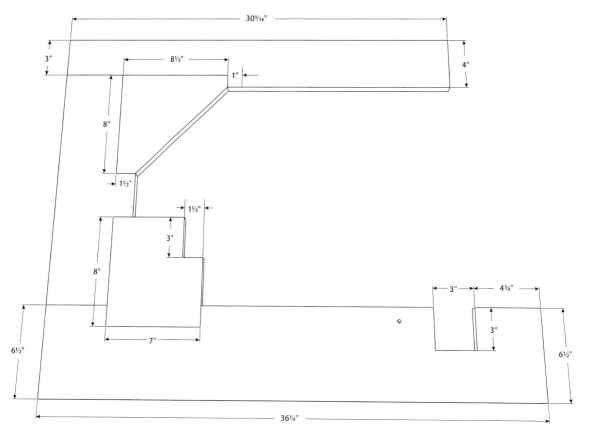

Frame Layer Two

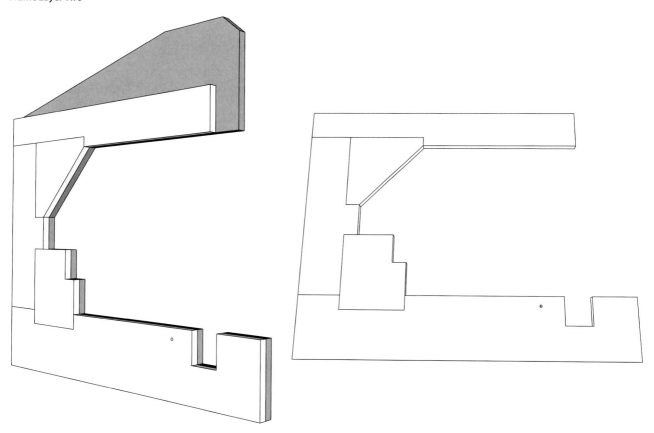

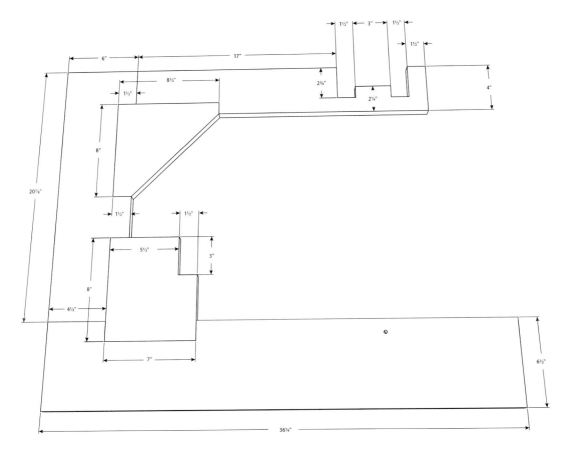

Frame Layer Three

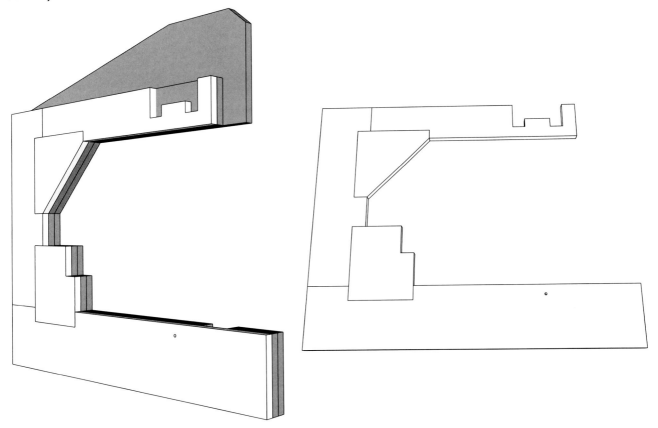

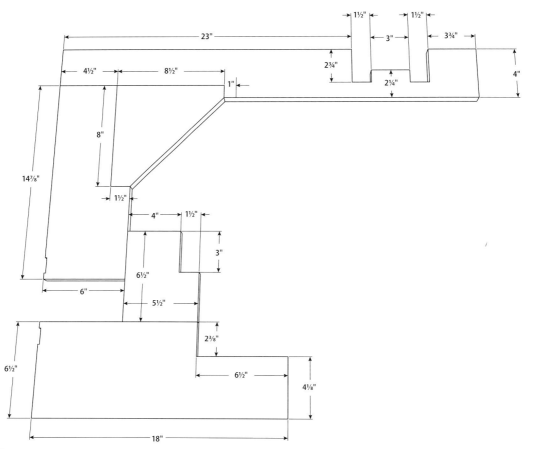

Frame Layer Four

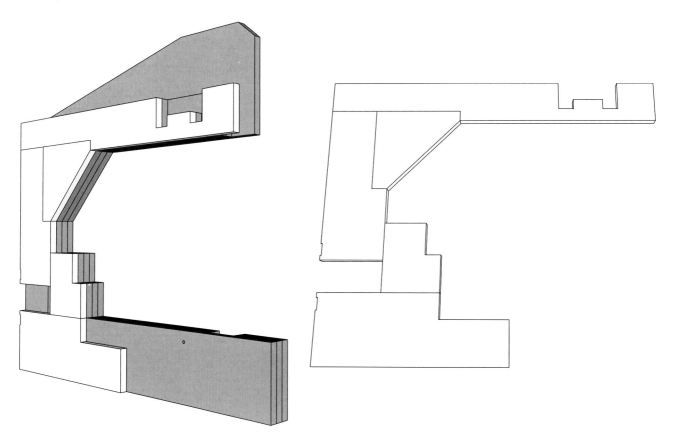

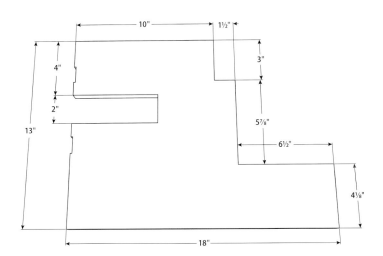

Frame Layer Five

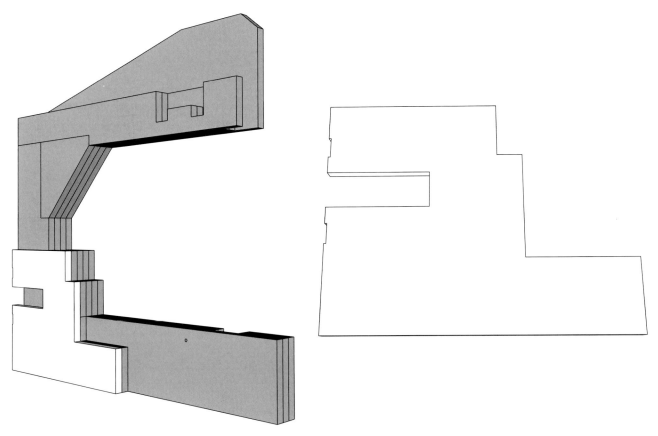

PART ONE: THE FRAME

The frame is constructed in layers glued together to form the mortises and cutouts you'll need for attaching parts later. Refer to the "Laminating the Frame" tip box on page 105 for more assistance.

Figure 1

STEP 1: Cut all of the frame layer parts using the included dimensions. Use care to make your cuts accurately.

STEP 2: Arrange the parts of your first layer on a flat surface. Coat them with glue, then coat the mating sides of each part of layer #2. Place the parts of layer #2 upon layer #1, carefully aligning each piece. Secure them with a few screws or nails.

STEP 3: Repeat the process with each of the five layers, always double-checking each part's alignment before adding fasteners.

STEP 4: Attach panel "F" to the spine of the frame using screws (**Figure 2**).

Figure 2

STEP 5: Glue parts G1 and G2 together into a sandwich, then glue them into the notch on the back of your frame. Cut the notches as shown in Figure 3. The larger of the two cutouts in parts G1 and G2 should face the spine of the frame (**Figure 4**).

STEP 6: Glue part H1 to part H3 so that the bottom edges align, then glue part H2 above H1, aligned with the top edge of H3 leaving about a ¾" between them. Use screws to attach the entire "H" assembly to the lower right end of the frame (**Figure 5**).

Figure 4

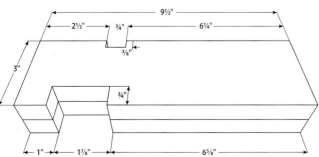
Figure 3

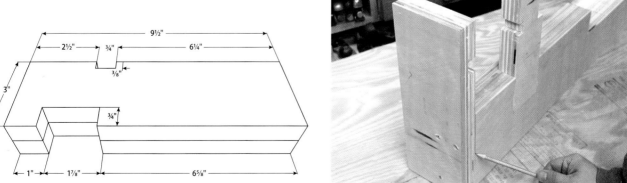
Figure 5

PART TWO:
THE WHEEL MOUNTS

STEP 7: Parts N1-N3 and M1-M3 can be made from layers of plywood laminated together as shown in the exploded view, or from hardwood as shown in **Figures 5 and 6**. The bottom line is, you need two blocks that are 2¼" thick, 1½" wide and 4½" tall. Bore a ⁵⁄₁₆" hole through the 2¼" side of each block, centered from side to side on that face and 1" from the block's end (**Figure 6**).

STEP 8: Part O should be hardwood, but you can laminate two pieces together to achieve the 1½" thickness. It should be 3" wide and 3¼" tall. Bore a ⁵⁄₁₆" hole through the 1½" side that is 1" from the top and 1⅛" from the back face (**Figure 6**).

STEP 9: Lay part O on the drill press table with the front face up (the face that the hole you just bored through the side is closest to). Measure from the top (the edge you positioned your hole 1" from in the last step), down 2¾" and centered from side to side. At this point, bore a ¾" hole (**Figure 7**).

STEP 10: Glue parts N and M into the recesses on the front, top of your frame. Position them so that the surfaces that the holes are closest to are facing out (**Figure 8**).

STEP 11: Slip part O between parts N and M, aligning the holes as shown in **Figure 9**. Insert a long ¼" bolt or piece of threaded rod through the holes in all three parts.

STEP 12: Flip part O up so you can see the frame behind it. Bore a hole through the frame that is roughly in the center and about 2¾" from the top edge. The hole should be large enough to fit a ¼" threaded insert (**Figure 10**).

STEP 13: Place a threaded insert into the hole behind part O and thread a carriage bolt through the insert and out the back of the frame (**Figure 11**).

Figure 6

Figure 7

Figure 8

Figure 9

Figure 10

Figure 11

Figure 12

Figure 13

Figure 14

STEP 14: For assembly EE you will need 3" x 3" and 2" x 3" blocks of hardwood. While the smaller block should be ¾" thick, the larger block must be slightly thinner than ¾" so that the assembly will slide freely when installed. Pass the block on it's edge between your table saw blade and fence to remove about ⅛" from its thickness. Use a proper push block for safety! Bore a ¾" hole through the center of the smaller block and a 1" hole through the center of the larger block. Place the smaller block on top of the larger and secure with glue **(Figure 12)**.

STEP 15: Bore a ⅜" hole through the EE assembly, directly in the center of the upper block and about ½" from the ¾" hole **(Figure 13)**.

Figure 15

STEP 16: Bore a ⁵⁄₁₆" hole through end of the assembly so that it intersects with the hole you just drilled **(Figure 13)**.

STEP 17: Use a chisel to enlarge the 1" hole on the bottom of your assembly to fit the head of a ¾" x 4" bolt **(Figure 14)**.

STEP 18: Insert a ¼" ID barrel into the ⅜" hole. Apply some epoxy to the end of a piece of ¼" threaded rod and insert it through the hole in the assembly's end and into the barrel nut. Allow time to cure **(Figure 15)**.

STEP 19: Cut six strips of hardwood that are 1½" wide, 6" long and ⅛" thick. Use wood with straight grain that runs down the length of the pieces. Bore a ¼" hole directly through the center of each. After the epoxy has cured, slip the rear wheel assembly into the slot in the frame's spine. Place four or five of the wood strips onto the end of the threaded rod. Place a couple of 1" x 1½" blocks of wood between the ends of the strips and the frame in the small recesses. Add a ¼" wing nut and a washer on the end **(Figure 16)**. Later, to install the rear wheel, slip a 1" steel spacer onto the ¾" x 4" bolt, then the rear wheel, and finally secure with a nut. Add washers between the spacer and hardwood block as needed to shim the wheel to the same plane as the upper wheel.

Figure 16

PART THREE: THE WHEELS & MOTOR

STEP 20: Cut out six 10" discs from ½" MDF. Take your time to ensure that you cut them as round as possible. You may wish to cut close to the compass line, then use disc or stationary belt sander to remove the rest of the material a little bit at a time until they are perfect. Glue the discs in pairs so you have three wheels of two ½" layers each (**Figures 17**).

STEP 21: Use a Forstner or spade bit that is the same diameter as the outside of your bearings to bore a hole in the center of each wheel. This hole should be only deep enough to allow your bearing flange to touch the surface of the wheel when you fasten it over the bearing. How deep the hole will have to be depends on your bearing's thickness and the depth that the flange nests over it. Bore a little bit, then check the fit, going deeper as needed. It may be best to perfect the depth on a scrap of wood, then set your drill press depth stop before boring into your wheels. It is important that you do not bore too deeply (**Figure 17 and 18**).

STEP 22: Bore the rest of the way through the center of each wheel with a 1" bit (**Figure 17**). Finally, mount a bearing in the center of each wheel using flanges (**Figure 18**). (Note: You can also make flanges from hardwood if you don't have steel ones.)

STEP 23: Set the wheels aside for now and cut a 9" disc from ¾" plywood. Bore a 1" hole, ⅛" deep in the center (**Figure 19**). Then bore the rest of the way through the center with a ¼" bit.

STEP 24: Slip a ¼" carriage bolt through the center hole and tighten it in place with a nut, then attach the assembly to your drill press chuck (**Figure 20**).

STEP 25: Using a rotary tool or power drill with a rasp-style bit, begin cutting a groove into the disc's edge as it spins in the drill press. A conical-shaped bit is preferred so you can form a "V" shaped groove to fit a link belt. Begin with very light pressure until you establish a kerf in the center of the disc's edge, then apply more pressure as you deepen the kerf (**Figure 20**). Stop from time to time to check the fit of your link belt, which should fit in the kerf without touching the bottom.

Figure 17

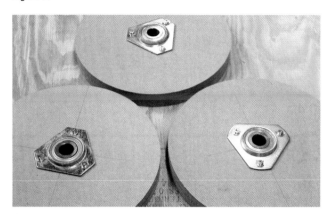

Figure 18

Figure 19

Figure 20

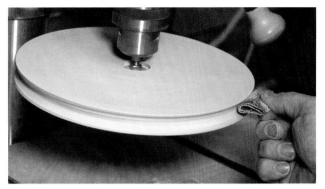

Figure 21

Figure 22

Figure 23

STEP 26: Clean up your wooden pulley and further shape the kerf with a folded piece of coarse sand paper **(Figure 21)**.

STEP 27: When you are satisfied with your kerf, remove the bolt. Install a 1" bit in your drill press and fit it into the slight recess you bored in the center of your disc before you shaped it. Bore the hole the rest of the way through the disc **(Figure 22)**.

STEP 28: Carefully align the wooden pulley with the center hole of one of the wheels. Secure them together with a pair of screws driven through the pulley and into the wheel. Do not use glue!

STEP 29: At this point you will have to bore a ¾" hole through the frame. It is important that the hole is straight, so if you must use a hand-held power drill, use a jig to be sure your drill is perpendicular to the face of the frame. You can also enlist the help of a friend to lift the frame onto your drill press table **(Figure 23)**. Clamp it in place and double-check the table alignment before boring the hole. It should be located on the lower horizontal portion of the frame, 1" from the top edge and 10¼" from the right side (inside face of part H) **(Figure 24)**. This should put the hole directly below the hole in the upper wheel mount above it.

STEP 30: Flip up the upper wheel mounting block (part O) so you can insert a ¾" bolt through a hole in the center with the threaded end facing out. Slip a ¾" long steel spacer onto the threaded end, then mount one of your rough wheels (which you will finish shaping then reinstall in Step #41), securing with a nut **(Figures 25 and 26)**.

STEP 31: Tighten the tilt adjustment bolt behind the mounting block to position the upper wheel in a horizontal position.

STEP 32: Slip a ¾" x 4" bolt through the bearing and out the pulley side of the wheel. Place a 2" steel spacer over the end of the bolt, then insert the bolt in the hole in your frame. Secure it finger tight with a nut on the back of the frame **(Figure 24)**.

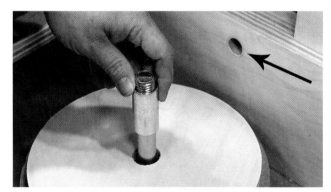

Figure 24

Figure 25

Figure 26

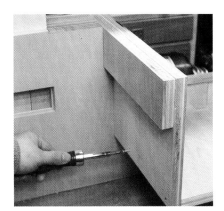

Figure 27

Figure 28

Figure 29

NOTE: The steel spacers should slip into the hole in the center of each wheel and touch the inner race of the bearing.

STEP 33: Attach the base panel to the bottom of the frame with screws. The back edge of the frame should be positioned 6" from the back edge of the bottom panel (**Figure 30**).

STEP 34: Parts I, J and Q make up the motor mount and should be installed now. These parts were included on your materials list, but you will have to cut away portions of parts I and J using the dimensions in **Figure 31**.

STEP 35: Attach part Q along the top edge of part I, then set them in their place on the frame. Panel J attaches along the bottom edge of I as shown. Be sure the entire assembly is perpendicular to the frame and secure with screws (**Figures 27 and 28**).

STEP 36: Use a straightedge to check the upper and lower wheels (**Figure 29**). You will likely have to add some washers behind the lower wheel between the spacer and the frame so that the two wheels are on the same plane.

Figure 30

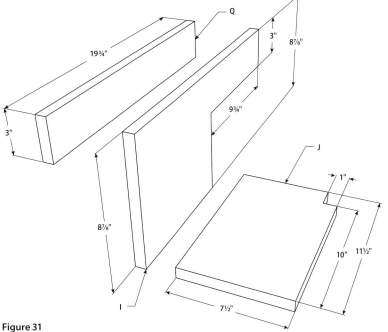

Figure 31

Figure 32

Figure 33

STEP 37: Sit the motor on its platform and align its pulley with the wooden pulley on the lower wheel. At this point the edge of the motor's base should be at the edge of the platform closest to the wheel. Adjust the length of your link belt to fit. **(Figures 32 and 33)**.

STEP 38: Install your belt, then slide the motor away from the wheel to tighten the belt. Mark the position of your mounting holes. If your motor base has elongated holes, mark on the end of the holes that is farthest from the wheel, which will give you the ability to tighten the belt even more if needed. Remove the motor, drill ¼" holes through the mounting platform and re-mount the motor with ¼" bolts **(Figure 33)**.

STEP 39: Before wiring your motor, check with someone qualified to do electrical work. It is best to route your wires behind the frame, attaching them to the back with staples. Remove the punch-outs on the back of a switch box, then mount it to the front of the frame in a convenient place. Bore holes through the frame so your wires can be fed from the back and through the punch-out holes in the switch box. Install a switch and a face plate **(Figures 34 and 35)**.

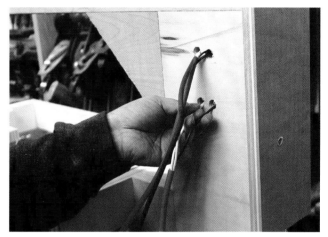

Figure 34

Figure 35

STEP 40: In the next two steps you'll finish shaping your three wheels, so refer back to Steps #19 and #32 and remove the rear wheel and the upper wheel for shaping (you'll reinstall them in Step #41). Put on a sanding mask; it's going to get dusty. Turn on the motor and use a rasp and coarse sandpaper to shape your lower wheel. You want to put a radius on the edge with its apex in the exact center of the wheel. The outer edges should be about ⅛" lower than the apex. **(Figure 36 and 37)**. Don't overdo it or you'll reduce the diameter of your wheel too much!

STEP 41: When your wheel is shaped, remove the wooden pulley and attach it to another wheel. Mount that wheel and pulley as before, replacing the one you just shaped. Repeat the whole process until all three wheels are shaped. Mount one finished wheel to the rear mounting block (Step #19 explains the proper spacer configuration for this mount), a second to the upper mounting block (Step #32 explains the proper spacer configuration for this mount) and leave the third attached to the pulley on the bottom.

Figure 36

Figure 37

Wobbly Wheels?

If your wheels wobble excessively it's likely that your bearings are the culprit. Be sure that the inner portion of the bearing does not have any play in it. High-quality bearings should be very precise. Another cause may be that the bearing is not registering flat on the wheel's surface because your drill press table was out of alignment when you bored the bearing recess. Or the bearing may not be perfectly centered on the wheel. If the vibration is so severe that it affects the saw's operation you will have to replace the bearings or remake the wheels.

Stumpy Nubs Woodworking — **PRO TIP**

PART FOUR:
BLADE GUIDES

STEP 42: Cut a 1½" x 2" block of ¾" thick hardwood. Mount a 2" piece of T-track along one edge. Bore a ⁵⁄₁₆" hole through the exact center of the space below the track (**Figure 38**).

STEP 43: On the other side, mount a second piece of track ⅛" from that same edge (**Figure 39**).

STEP 44: Place this assembly onto a ¾" thick scrap. Cut a piece 3½" x 1½". Stand that one on end next to the assembly you just made and mark the point shown in **Figure 40**.

STEP 45: Position the assembly on your bench so that the track that is flush with the edge is on the top left. Lay the 3½" long piece on it so that it is flush with the back end and the point you marked is aligned with the left edge of the block as shown in **Figure 41**. Secure with screws and glue.

STEP 46: Attach a 2½"-long piece of T-track to the edge of the upper block as shown in **Figure 42**.

STEP 47: Cut a block of ¾"-thick hardwood to 4" x 1⅞" Attach a 3" piece of T-track ¾" from one of the long edges and touching the short edge as shown in **Figure 43**.

STEP 48: Place the larger assembly on top of the track you just mounted as shown in **Figure 44**. Use a 1"-long, ¼" machine screw and a T-track nut to secure them together.

Figure 38

Figure 39

Figure 40

Figure 41

Figure 42

Figure 43

Figure 44

STEP 49: Place a bearing and two washers (between the bearing and track) on the T-track as shown in **Figure 45**, using a ¼" flat-head machine screw and a T-nut to secure them.

STEP 50: Cut four T-nuts just to the left of the hole creating a shorter end (**Figure 46**).

STEP 51: Pare away the corner of the block shown in **Figure 45** with a chisel. This will provide clearance for the bearings.

STEP 52: Attach a pair of bearings to the front T-track as shown in **Figure 47**, using two of the cut nuts. Face the cut ends toward the center of the track so you can place the two bearings closer to each other. Insert one washer between each bearing and the track.

STEP 53: Attach the lower blade-guide assembly in the larger of the two notches in part G on the band saw frame. Use only screws to hold it in place (**Figure 48**).

Figure 45

Figure 46

Figure 47

Figure 48

Figure 49

Skate Bearings

A great place to get bearings for this project is an old pair of in-line roller skates. You can find them at yard sales and flea markets for a few bucks and one pair of skates will yield 16 bearings (2 per wheel)! The size of the hole in the center may vary, but if you use flat-head machine screws, the taper beneath the head will center the bearing as you tighten it. You may have to cut through the wheel to get at the bearings inside. These bearings are also useful for all sorts of other projects, so whenever you see a cheap pair of skates, grab them!

Stumpy Nubs Woodworking
PRO TIP

Figure 50

Figure 51

STEP 54: Cut a 12" long piece of hardwood that is 1½" thick and 1½" wide. You can laminate two ¾" pieces together to achieve the required thickness.

STEP 55: Cut the two blocks shown in **Figure 52** from ¾"-thick hardwood. The dado is ¼" deep and just wide enough for a piece of T-track to slip inside (¾"). Do not cut the dado too wide!

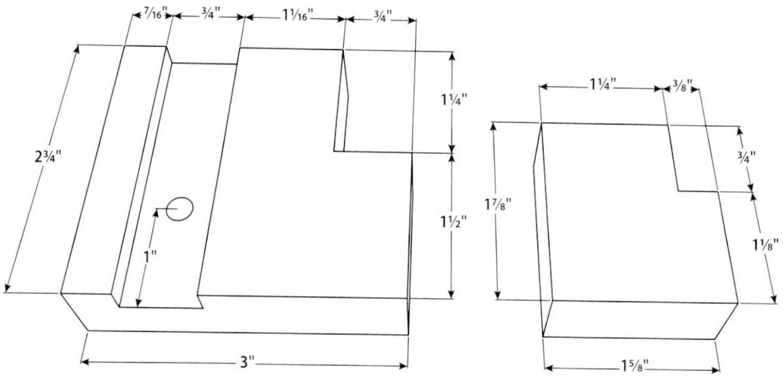

STEP 56: Cut another dado in the end of your 12"-long piece, ⁷⁄₁₆" from one of the edges and ⅛" deep. Use a push block to help support the base and keep the part perpendicular to the table as you cut (**Figure 49**).

Figure 52

STEP 57: Place a 2¾"-long piece of T-track in the slot on the end of the long part, securing with screws (**Figure 50**).

STEP 58: Bore a ⁵⁄₁₆" hole directly in the center of the larger block's groove, 1" from the edge as shown in **Figures 50 and 52**.

STEP 59: Attach the smaller block to the larger with screws as shown in **Figure 51**.

STEP 60: Attach a 1⅝" piece of T-track to the face of the smaller block as shown in **Figure 53**.

STEP 61: Attach the assembly to the bottom of the 12- long piece as shown in **Figure 54**. The T-track will fit in the groove and a 1" machine screw passes through the hole in the assembly and into a T-nut within the track. This allows you to adjust the upper blade-guide assembly to accommodate various blade widths. You may use a washer or two if the machine screw bottoms out before it's tight.

Figure 53

Figure 54

STEP 62: Locate part M from your materials list. You will be boring two holes that are large enough to fit a pair of ¼" threaded inserts. Both holes are 1" from the left edge, the first is 1" from the bottom and the second 4" above that **(Figure 55)**.

STEP 63: Fit inserts in the holes as shown in **Figure 55**. Thread a 2"-long ¼" carriage bolt into each insert so that the head is on the insert side. Place a ¼" nut and a ¼" knob on the end of each bolt. Snug the nuts tightly against the knobs **(Figure 56)**.

STEP 64: Install part M as shown in **Figure 57**. Drive a pair of screws through the back panel and into the edge of part M, and two more through the face of the part and into the frame to the left of the knobs.

STEP 65: Slide the shaft of your new upper blade-guide assembly into the cavity behind part M, tightening the knobs to hold it in place **(Figure 58)**.

STEP 66: If you haven't already, re-install the upper and lower wheels. Be sure that they are on the same plane as before.

STEP 67: Install the rear wheel using a 1" spacer (refer back to Step #19). Check to see if it is on the same plane as the upper wheel using a straight edge. Shim with washers between the spacer and the frame as needed.

Figure 55

Figure 56

Figure 57

Figure 58

Choosing a Band Saw Blade

Band saw blades come in a variety of styles, and this space isn't big enough to get into tooth shape and spacing, etc. Let's stick to the basics: length and width. This saw is designed to fit a 104" blade, but there is enough room for adjustment to allow some leeway there. While the saw likely will support a wider blade, I'd stick to ⅜" or narrower. Wider blades require a lot more tension, which will challenge any wooden frame's strength, while narrow blades flex around the 10" wheels better.

Stumpy Nubs Woodworking
PRO TIP

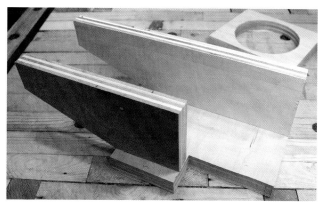

Figure 59

PART FIVE:
DUST COLLECTION

STEP 68: The parts of the dust-collection assembly were included in the materials list, but you may use the dimensions below to cut the angles, etc. **(Figure 60)**.

STEP 69: The hole in part AA should fit the dust-collection fitting on the end of your hose snugly.

STEP 70: Attach parts Y and Z to part BB as shown in **Figure 59** using glue and brad nails.

STEP 71: Attach parts X, AA and CC as shown in **Figure 61** using glue and brad nails.

Figure 61

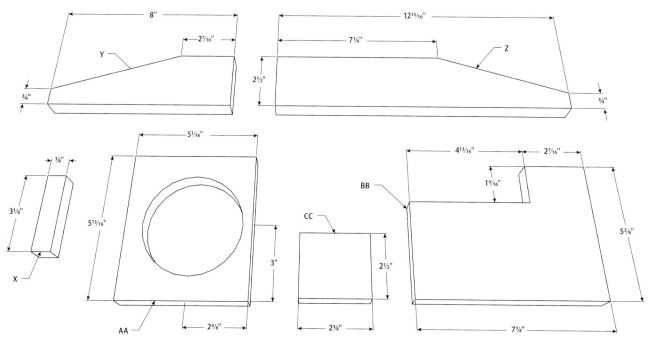

Figure 60

STEP 72: To enhance your dust collection you may wish to caulk the seams, but the benefits will be minimal **(Figure 62)**.

STEP 73: Slip the dust-collection assembly into the notches in the frame **(Figures 63 and 64)**.

STEP 74: Install your blade. Adjust the guide bearings so that they are as close to the blade as possible without touching the blade when you turn the wheels by hand. Test the blade's tracking manually, tightening the bolt behind the upper wheel mount to make adjustments before turning on the saw for the first time.

Figure 62

Figure 63

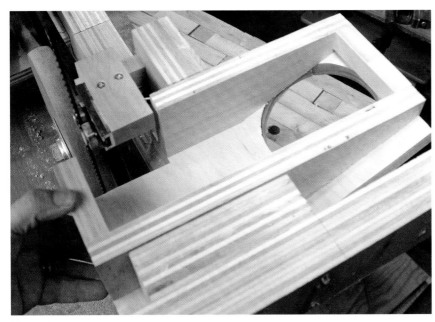

Figure 64

PART SIX: THE SLIDING TABLE

STEP 75: Laminate parts S1 and S2 together with glue. Attach them to outside of part H3 on the right side of the frame as shown in **Figure 65**. The S parts should protrude 6" behind the back edge of part H3. Be sure that they are at a 90° angle to each other and the top edges are flush before securing with screws.

STEP 76: Measure from the outside (right) edge of the S parts (which we'll call the "right table support" now) to the blade. Transfer this measurement to the front (33¼" long) edge of the lower table panel (part U). Bore a ⅜" hole at that point, 1½" deep into the edge of the panel **(Figure 66)**.

STEP 77: Place the panel on your table saw with the hole facing the blade. Because the hole is not centered on the edge, there is more distance to the corner on one side of the hole than the other. You should have the greater distance on your right. Set your fence to cut a kerf directly through the center of the hole. Raise your blade to its highest position and cut into the center of your panel 10½" before stopping. Turn off the saw before removing the panel **(Figure 67)**. This is your "lower table panel."

STEP 78: Do not move the table saw's fence. Locate panel W from your materials list. It should be 25" wide, which is intentionally oversized. Cut it narrower using the same fence position from the last step. This is your "upper table panel."

STEP 79: Measure from the kerf in the "lower table panel" to the edge closest to it. Trim panel V to that width as it was also intentionally oversized on the materials list. This is your "sliding table panel" **(Figure 68)**.

STEP 80: Install a dado set in your saw, or bit in your router table that is the same width as your T-track. Raise the cutter exactly half the thickness of the track. (Use some scrap material to make a few test cuts to ensure that the width and depth of the groove is precise.) Set your fence 1" from the cutter and cut a groove in the face of your lower table panel as shown in **Figure 68**.

STEP 81: Without moving the fence, cut a groove along the edge of the sliding table panel as shown in **Figure 68**.

STEP 82: Adjust the fence to 6" from the cutter and run both panels again, with the same faces down. This will create two grooves in each that are in the same position **(Figure 68)**.

Figure 65

Figure 66

Figure 67

Figure 68

STEP 83: Raise your cutter to the full thickness of your T-track now. Cut a pair of grooves in the opposite side of the sliding table panel. Their location should be just between the grooves below them as shown in **Figure 69**. Note: The position of your grooves may be slightly different from those in the images depending on where your saw blade was located, which determined the width of your panels.

STEP 84: Install T-track in the grooves in the lower table panel, and in those in the sliding table panel. Your two panels should nest together and slide freely as shown in **Figure 70**.

STEP 85: Glue the upper table panel on top of the lower table panel, aligning it along the left and front edges. **(Figure 71)**

STEP 86: Use screws to attach the entire table assembly to the frame's table supports. Countersink the screw heads. The screws on the right side of the table should be beneath the sliding table panel **(Figure 72)**.

Figure 69

Figure 70

Figure 71

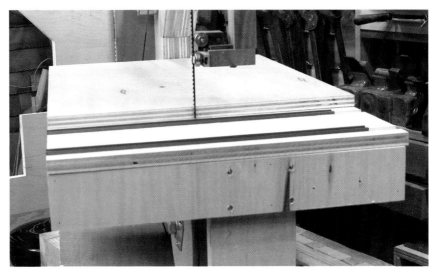

Figure 72

Figure 73

Figure 74

STEP 87: As you fasten the left side of your table assembly to the supports, use a combination square to ensure that your sliding table is running parallel to the blade. Set your square so that the end of the rule touches the blade when the table is in the furthest forward position **(Figure 73)**. Then see if it also touches it when you slide the table to the back position **(Figure 74)**. The table supports on the right side will flex a bit, so push on the left front corner of the entire table assembly to adjust its alignment until your ruler test achieves the proper results. Then use screws to fasten the left edge of the table assembly as described in the previous step.

STEP 88: The front cover is optional, but it's a good safety feature. You can cut it from plywood using the dimensions in **Figure 77** as a guide, but you may have to make some modifications to fit your saw. So check before you cut! Mount the cover with hinges on the left side of the saw **(Figure 75)**.

STEP 89: You will have to attach two small panels to the right edge of your cover as seen in **Figure 76**. The upper panel is 4⅛" wide, and the lower is 2" wide. Modify yours if needed so that they both touch the saw frame when the cover is closed. You may also attach latches to these panels and the mating points on the frame if needed to keep the cover closed.

NOTE: I didn't originally designed this saw to have a cover. I wanted to see the wheels spin! But all of that exposed blade does looks a little scary, and the safety folks said I should cover it up. This created a problem – you have to open the cover to turn the saw on! You may be fine with that, but I spent some time coming up with a couple of solutions which you can retrofit to your saw. They are found in the free online video content on our website (See the Pro Tip on page 127).

STEP 90: Cut the threaded portion off of a ⅜" bolt. This will be used as a pin to keep the table flat. Insert in after everything is assembled and the blade is installed **(Figure 78)**.

Figure 75

Figure 76

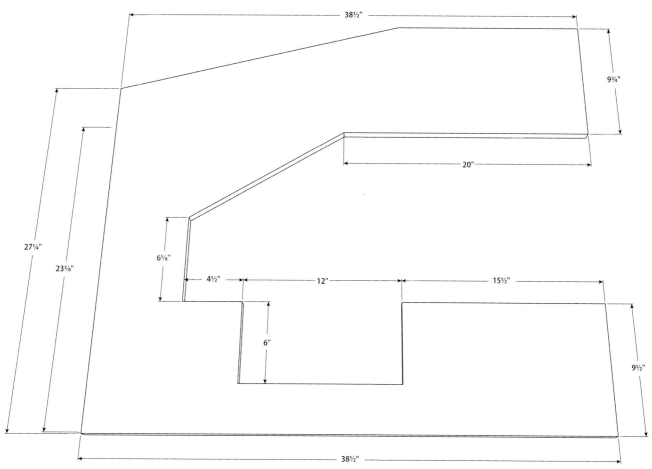

Figure 77

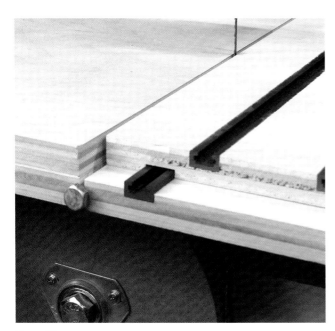

Figure 78

Important:
Before You Turn It On...

- Are all three wheel-mount bolts tight?

- Are all three wheels shimmed to the same plane?

- Is the switch wired properly?

- Is the blade tracking properly?

- Is the cover attached and closed?

We've produced some bonus video content to help you get the most out of your new band saw. We show you how to tune it up, how to use the sliding table, even how to build a fence. You should definitely check it out:

stumpynubs.com/homemade-tools/html

Stumpy Nubs Woodworking
PRO TIP

Table Saw Fence

The next three projects go together like mashed potatoes and gravy. You see, over the years that we've produced our online woodworking show, I've found that many woodworkers are held back by their table saws. Not everyone can afford a heavy-duty saw, in fact a lot of weekend woodworkers try to get by with cheap benchtop machines that have a way of making their precious shop time frustrating and even dangerous. It's a problem that has to be fixed. I was thinking of starting a telethon. We could have some woodworkers looking sadly into the camera, maybe get a celebrity or two to sing a song. People could call in pledges and we'd use the cash to buy good table saws for all! If it works for puppies and Jerry Lewis, why not for us craftsmen?

But let's face facts: we're going to have to solve this problem ourselves. So I'm doing my part by designing home-made accessories that can make any table saw much more useable. And because the biggest disappointment anyone who buys a cheap saw faces is the rickety fence, that's just where we'll start.

The concept is simple – a fence that is easy to build, versatile and, most of all, accurate. I hate having to use a measuring tape to check the front and rear of the saw blade to make sure the fence is parallel before every cut. So I designed this one with a self-squaring mechanism that is as simple as twisting a knob. When you do, a beveled strip is pulled into a mating channel along the rail, locking the fence in place and squaring it at the same time. Those rails are another important innovation. They're made from hardwood rather than expensive steel tubing. You have the option of both front and rear rails if you wish to mount an extension table or a router between them. And the fence itself incorporates a unique micro-adjustable sliding carriage feature that is fantastic for dialing in precise cuts.

You've likely noticed the photo below doesn't look like your typical table saw fence. That's because it's inspired by the European design which is much shorter than our big American T-style units. They prefer their fences to only extend to the center of the saw blade because it reduces the risk of kickback when a workpiece is caught between a long fence and the blade. Of course I also designed an extension for those who prefer the longer style. In fact, I designed my fence to accept a variety of auxiliary attachments that are only limited by your imagination. And did I mention there's a built-in pencil holder?

An excellent replacement for that temperamental fence that came with your table saw, this one is micro-adjustable and more!

Table Saw Fence

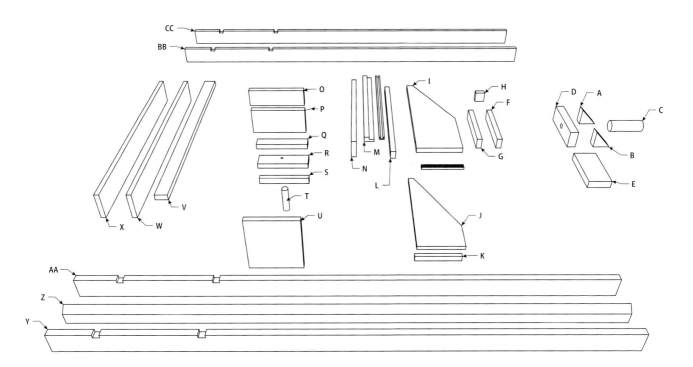

Materials List

QTY	PART	REFERENCE	DIMENSIONS	STOCK
1	Micro-adjuster bracket	A & B	1½" x 1½"	¾" plywood
1	Micro-adjuster face	D	4¾" x 1½"	¾" plywood
1	Micro-adjuster base	E	4¾" x 2¼"	¾" plywood
2	Parts holder sides	F & G	8⁷⁄₁₆" x 1½"	¾" plywood
1	Parts holder end	H	1½" x 1½"	¾" plywood
1	Carriage base panel	I	19½" x 7"	¾" plywood
1	Base panel	J	20¼" x 9"	¾" plywood
1	Carriage inner fence	L	19½" x 1⅛"	¾" plywood
1	Carriage upper fence	M	19½" x 1½"	¾" plywood
1	Carriage outer fence	N	19½" x 2⅝"	¾" plywood
1	Upper front panel	O	7½" x 2¼"	¾" plywood
1	Center front panel	P	7½" x 3½"	¾" plywood
1	Lock pressure plate	Q	7½" x 1½"	¾" plywood
1	Lock plate	R	7½" x 2¼"	¾" plywood
1	Lower front panel	S	7½" x 1"	¾" plywood
1	Outer front panel	U	7½" x 8¼"	¾" plywood
2	Handles	C & T	6" long	1¼" hardwood dowel
1	Lock wedge	K	9" x 2"	¾" hardwood
2	Front rails	Y & AA	60" x 2½"	¾" hardwood
1	Front beveled rail	Z	60" x 2⅛"	¾" hardwood
OPTIONAL MATERIALS				
1	Extension upper panel	V	30" x 2"	¾" plywood
1	Extension face panels	W & X	30" x 4¼"	¾" plywood
2	Rear rails	BB & CC	60" x 2½"	¾" hardwood

Additional Hardware

About 27" of T-track
2 ¼" x 1½" T-track bolts
3 ¼" wing nuts and washers
2 1.4" acorn style cap nuts
2 ¼" x 3" hanger bolts
2 ¼" threaded insert or T-nut
3 #8 1½" pan-head sheet metal screws
Misc., carriage bolts for mounting to saw
5' self adhesive measuring tape
3M non-skid grip tape
PVC slick tape or similar material

PART ONE: THE FENCE

STEP 1: Bore a ⁵⁄₁₆" hole in the center of part D, about 1" from an edge and insert a ¼" threaded T-nut as shown in **Figure 1**.

STEP 2: Use glue to attach part D to the edge of part E as shown in **Figure 2**.

STEP 3: The materials list included a 1½" square from which you will cut your two micro-adjuster brackets (A and B). Cut it diagonally through the center. You may also wish to trim the points as shown in **Figure 3**, then assemble as illustrated.

STEP 4: Gather your carriage parts **(Figure 4)**. Place panel I on your bench with one of the short ends facing you. Measure 8⁷⁄₁₆" up the right side, then measure 1" across the top edge from the left to right. Connect the two points with a straight line, then cut along that line, forming the shape seen in **Figure 4**.

STEP 5: Cut a dado 2" from the end of panel I. The dado should be ⅜" deep and as wide as your T-track. Do not cut it too wide! It is critical that a T-track slides smoothly within the dado without any side-to-side wobble! So cut carefully!

STEP 6: Use glue and brad nails to attach the three sides of the carriage parts holder as shown in **Figure 6**.

STEP 7: Panel J must be cut in a similar manner as you did panel I. The time measure 5½" up the long side, and 1" across the top. Connect with a line and cut as before.

STEP 8: Attach part O to the edge of J as shown in **Figure 7**.

Figure 1

Figure 2

Figure 3

Figure 4

Figure 5

Figure 6

Figure 7

Figure 8

Figure 9

Figure 10

STEP 9: Attach part U as shown in **Figure 8**.

STEP 10: Stand the assembly on end, and attach part P as shown in **Figure 9**.

STEP 11: Bore a ⁵⁄₁₆" hole in part R, centered along its length and about 1½" from one of the long edges. Insert a ¼" threaded T-nut as shown in **Figure 10**.

STEP 12: The edge of part R that you measured from before boring your hole is the one that butts against panel U as shown in **Figure 11**, with part S attached below it.

Figure 11

Too Much Wobble in Your Groove?

Mistakes happen! If you find that the T-track fits too loosely in your upper carriage's groove, you have to fix it or else the entire fence will be inaccurate. No problem, just glue a strip of wood in the offending dado. After it's dry, recut as before except with more care this time. It's better to cut it undersized, then gradually make it wider, checking the fit repeatedly. Everything depends on the accuracy of that cut!

Stumpy Nubs Woodworking
PRO TIP

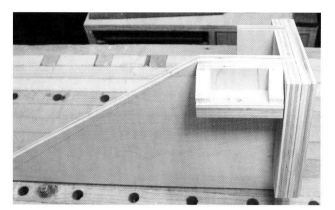

Figure 12

Figure 13

Figure 14

Figure 15

STEP 13: Attach the assembly from steps 1-2 to panel J as shown **Figure 12**, gluing both the bottom and side surfaces. You can use this assembly to square up the front of the fence. Clamp as shown in **Figure 13** until dry.

STEP 14: Attach a 6" piece of T-track as shown in **Figure 14.** It should be 2" from and perfectly parallel to the rear panels of the assembly. Be careful while installing screws so the tapered heads don't force the track out of alignment!

STEP 15: You should be able to lay your upper carriage assembly (panel I) on top so that the T-track rides in the dado you cut in Step 5. The carriage should slide freely back and forth. If the edge of the carriage drags against the front panels, trim it slightly using a table saw miter gauge as shown in **Figure 15**.

STEP 16: Bore a ⁵⁄₁₆" hole through panel I directly in the center of the groove on the underside. Position the hole 1½" from the parts holder as shown in **Figure 15**.

STEP 17: To attach the upper carriage you will need a 1½"-long x ¼" T-bolt, a wing nut and a washer. **(Figure 16)**.

STEP 18: The head of the bolt slips into the track and is secured with the washer and wing nut above panel I as shown in **Figure 17**.

Figure 16

Figure 17

Figure 18

Figure 19

Figure 20

Figure 21

STEP 19: The two handles on your materials list can be any length you are comfortable with. Drill a hole in the end of each to fit the screw thread end in your ¼" hanger bolts **(Figure 18)**. Make the holes deep enough that the entire thread will fit inside. Before you screw the bolts in, liberally apply some epoxy to the threads.

STEP 20: One handle threads into the micro-adjuster assembly on the top of the carriage **(Figure 19)** while the other fits beneath the fence **(Figure 25)**. Epoxy ¼" acorn cap nuts on the ends of both handles after you install them.

STEP 21: Part K was intentionally oversized on the materials list. This is to make it safer to cut a 45° bevel on the edge. After cutting the bevel, trim off the sharp edge, then rip the piece to ⅞" **(Figures 20 and 21)**.

STEP 22: Place the ruler from your combination square and a ¾"-thick scrap of wood between part K and the rear panels on the underside of panel J as shown in **Figure 22**. Use a pencil to mark the position of park K, then remove the ruler and scrap piece.

STEP 23: Clamp part K in the position you marked, using a square to ensure that it is perfectly square to the side of panel J **(Figure 23)**. Bore pilot holes and secure with pan-head screws (countersink the heads) from the other side of panel J **(Figure 24)**.

Figure 22

Figure 23

Figure 24

Figure 25

Figure 26

Figure 27

STEP 24: Bore a ½" hole in the center of part Q, then it on top of the acorn nut beneath the fence as shown in **Figure 25**. You may also wish to apply some grip tape to the top side of part Q as well (See box).

STEP 25: Set the entire fence assembly so that the end hangs off your bench as shown in **Figure 26**. Attach strip L as illustrated in the photo. Use glue to secure it along the edge of panel I.

STEP 26: You will have to cut a rabbet along the edge of strip M that is as wide and deep as your T-track. The track must lie flat within the rabbet facing up as shown in **Figure 27**, with the top flush with the surface of strip M. Secure with screws.

STEP 27: Fasten the track and strip M to the edge of part N as shown in **Figure 28**.

STEP 28: Use screws with countersunk heads to attach the assembly to your fence as shown in **Figure 29**.

A Work in Progress

The T-track on the top of this fence makes it possible to add any number of attachments. For example, a longer fence extension, assembled from optional parts V, W and X in the materials list, can be used for greater accuracy while cutting large panels. Other accessories such as feather boards and hold-downs can be made to fit as well. Keep an eye on **stumpynubs.com/homemade-tools** as we develop even more attachment ideas!

Stumpy Nubs Woodworking
PRO TIP

Figure 28

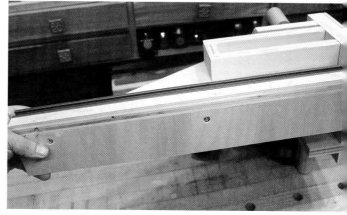
Figure 29

PART TWO: THE RAILS

STEP 29: The front fence rail is made up of three layers of ¾"-thick hardwood. I made mine 5' long, but you could really do any length you like as long as you have some sort of support. Rip them to width according to the materials list.

STEP 30: Rail Z should be beveled at 45° along one edge, then ripped to the final width of 2⅛".

STEP 31: The three layers will be mounted individually. Rail AA must be attached to the front of your table saw. Use a square to draw lines across the rail at the center of each hole (**Figure 30**). Then set the square body on the top of the saw table, extending the ruler so that the corner is in the center of one hole (**Figure 31**). Finally, lay the square's body on the top edge of your rail and mark with a pencil where the end of the ruler crosses each of your lines (**Figure 32**).

STEP 32: Use a ⅞" bit to bore a ⅜"-deep hole at each point, then a 5⁄16" bit to bore the rest of the way through. Be sure you are drilling perpendicular to the rail's face. This will provide a recess for the heads of your carriage bolts to set below the surface (**Figure 33**).

STEP 33: Use ¼" carriage bolts with nuts and lock washers to attach the fence rail to the front of your saw. Check with a straight edge to ensure that the rail is level with the top.

Figure 30

Figure 31

Figure 32

Figure 33

Figure 34

Leave Room for Adjustment

¼" carriage bolts are used to mount the rail to the front of your saw because they are usually smaller than the existing holes, which allows you room to adjust. If your saw's holes are smaller than 7⁄16", then you should bore larger holes in your rail to give you room to adjust using those holes instead.

Stumpy Nubs Woodworking
PRO TIP

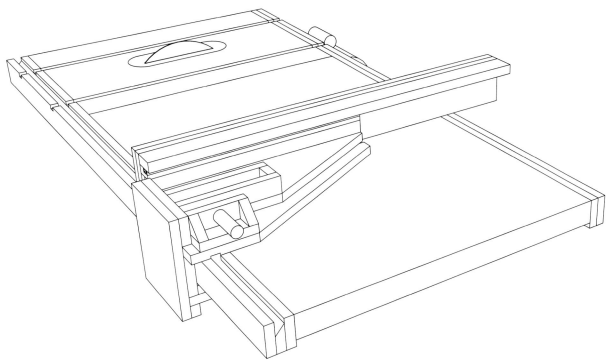

Figure 35

STEP 34: Keeping the rails straight will require some sort of extension table that is the same width as the saw. A double layer of plywood or MDF will work nicely. If you are planning to install such a table **(Figure 35)**, you will have to repeat the process above to mount a second rail (BB) to the opposite side of your saw. You can then mount the table between them by driving screws through both rails into the edges. Finally, add a third rail (CC) to the rear, creating a double layer for strength. Depending on the weight of your table, you may also wish to attach some sort of supporting legs to the end so the saw will not tip.

STEP 35: If your saw is mounted in our Table Saw Workstation, you won't need to use rear rails. Drive screws through the face to rail AA down its length to secure it to the front of the bench. Check to see that it remains flat as you do so. If the front of your bench is not straight, the rail may bend. In that case you will have to insert a few shims to keep it straight **(Figure 36)**.

STEP 36: However you choose to mount your fence, all screws must be countersunk flush with the surface **(Figure 37)**.

Figure 36

Figure 37

Figure 38

Figure 39

Figure 40

STEP 37: Mount beveled rail Z to the front rail (AA) using screws all down the length. Be sure that the bottom edges of both rails align, and that the bevel slopes away from the saw **(Figure 38)**.

STEP 38: Mount the final rail (Y) to the front of rails AA and Z. You will have to drive your screws into the face of the rail lower than before so that they do not break through above the bevel in rail Z. Use screws that are long enough to pass through all three rails and ensure that rail Y is not higher than rail AA **(Figure 39)**.

STEP 39: After all three rails are mounted (and the rear rail if applicable) you will have to use a handsaw and chisel to cut notches in all but the beveled rail so that the saw's miter slots are not obstructed **(Figure 35)**.

STEP 40: It is a good idea to apply some high quality non-skid tape to the top of part Q. 3M is best because the granules are less likely to come off over time **(Figure 40 and 41)**.

Figure 41

STEP 41: It's also a good idea to apply few strips of PVC glide tape to the underside of the fence.

STEP 42: A self-adhesive measuring tape should be applied to the top of the rail. Place a straightedge against your saw blade so that it is not touching the teeth **(Figure 42)**. Use a pencil to draw a line where the edge crosses the front rail. Apply your measuring tape so that the zero point is on that line **(Figure 43)**.

NOTE: Using a blade of a different thickness, for example thin-kerf as opposed to full-kerf, will change your zero point on most saws. If you use both types of blades, consider adding a second tape to the top of the other rail so you have one for thin kerf blades, and one for full kerf blades.

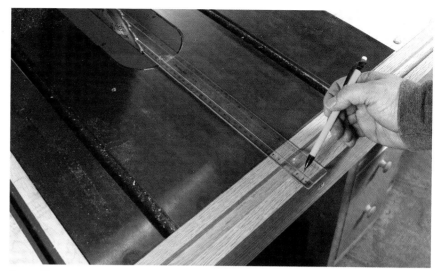

Figure 42

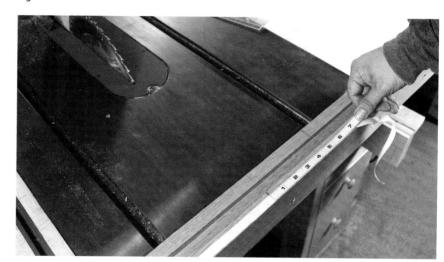

Figure 43

Tuning and Using Your Fence

The operation of this fence is simple. Tightening the knob on the bottom pulls the fence down, forcing the beveled block against the beveled portion of the fence, self squaring the whole thing. If you find that your fence bottoms out on the top of the rails before this happens, add some shims above the beveled block you installed in Step #25. If your fence is not perfectly parallel to your saw's miter slots, shim behind the fence face you installed in Step #30. As long as that face is aligned, any auxiliary fence you add will be as well. Micro-adjusting the fence is simply a matter of loosening the wing nut on top and turning the knob on your right. Re-tighten the wing nut before making a cut. If the sliding portion of the fence doesn't remain aligned as it moves on the T-track beneath, your slot was cut too wide. Refer to the box entitled "Too Much Wobble in Your Groove?" for a remedy. And, of course, be sure to visit our website for additional video content to help you get the most out of your new fence!
stumpynubs.com/homemade-tools/html

Stumpy Nubs Woodworking
PRO TIP

Sliding Crosscut Table

Those Europeans have been kicking our American butts for years when it comes to table saws, and most of us never knew it. When I started woodworking I thought all table saws were the same noisy man killers that made ragged cuts through wood and the occasional finger. Little did I know there was a whole other world across the pond! I discovered this strange universe of table saw goodness years ago during a visit to the old country. There I found a mysterious land full of people speaking strange languages. Their food wasn't great, but their saws were exquisite. They had wonderful features like stubby fences and sliding tables, features that were said to increase accuracy and reduce accidents. I knew I had to bring these innovations back home and incorporate them into my own designs.

The first features I borrowed from our European brethren went into my homemade table saw fence, which you may have already met in a previous chapter. But this one is the granddaddy of them all, a table saw jig so big that it needs its own leg for extra support! It's an attachment that replaces one of the saw's wings, adding a sliding surface that can replace your miter gauge. Why would you replace your handy-dandy miter gauge with a big sliding surface? I'm so glad you asked!

You see, a sliding table offers far greater capacity than the typical miter gauge. Squaring up wide panels is as simple as tea and biscuits. Cutting miters, making repeated cuts – everything you used to do with your miter gauge – is more accurate because the workpiece isn't sliding across the top of the saw. The work stays put as the top itself moves. This reduces the chance for slippage.

Of course, I'm not the first to attempt a homemade version. But where this one shines is in the way the overall design has been simplified. No bearings or sliders, just a simple tracking system that is very easy to build. The fence itself can be adjusted to any angle, it features a sacrificial face, and a moveable stop for making repeated cuts. When you want it out of the way it comes off quickly and the table locks in a stationary position. The best part is that this table is designed for mounting on our big table saw workstation project or, with the optional base unit that includes a handy storage drawer, you can mount it to the side of most free-standing table saws.

It's high time we stood up as Americans and said enough to table saw tyranny! The Europeans have been laughing at our table saws with their non-sliding tops for far too long! Today we conquer our table saws, tomorrow – the world!

Make crosscuts like a pro – even with sheet goods – with this European-style sliding table that attaches to the side of your saw!

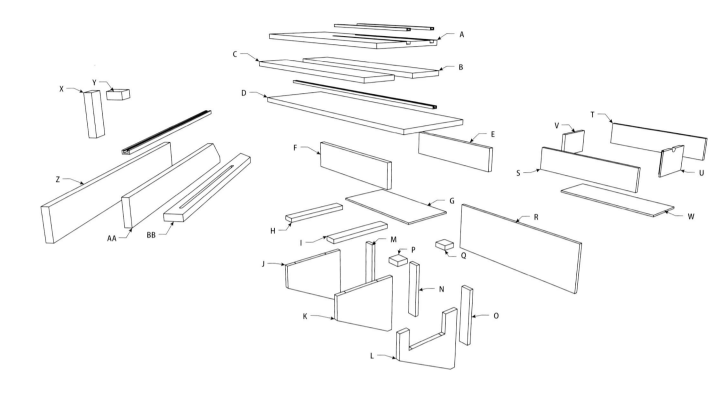

Materials List

QTY	PART	REFERENCE	DIMENSIONS	STOCK
1	Upper table surface panel	A	30" x 12"	¾" plywood
2	Upper table slide panels	B & C	30" x 5⅝"	¾" plywood
1	Lower table panel	D	37½" x 12"	¾" plywood
1	Stop back	X	4⅛" x 1½"	¾" plywood
1	Stop top	Y	1½" x 1½"	¾" plywood
1	Fence front panel	Z	3⅜" x 26½"	¾" plywood
1	Fence rear panel	AA	3" x 25¾"	¾" plywood
1	Fence bottom panel	BB	2" x 25¾"	¾" plywood
OPTIONAL SAW MOUNT MATERIALS:				
2	Lower table side panels	E & F	16¼" x 3¾"	¾" plywood
2	Bracket upper mounts	H & I	2" x 12"	¾" plywood
2	Solid brackets	J & K	10½" x 12¾"	¾" plywood
1	Cutout bracket	L	10½" x 12¾"	¾" plywood
3	Bracket rear mounts	M-O	2" x 10½"	¾" plywood
2	Bracket upper mounts	P & Q	2" x 2"	¾" plywood
1	Saw mounting panel	R	33¼" x 11"	¾" plywood
2	Drawer side panels	S & T	16" x 3⁷⁄₁₆"	¾" plywood
1	Drawer front	U	3¹¹⁄₁₆" x 6⅜"	¾" plywood
1	Drawer back	V	3⁷⁄₁₆" x 5⅜"	¾" plywood
1	Drawer bottom	W	16" x 6⅜"	¼" MDF
1	Lower table bottom panel	G	15½" x 8"	¼" MDF

Additional Hardware

3   36" lengths of T-track
3   ¼" x 1½" T-track bolts
1   ¼" T-track nut
1   1¼" long x ¼" flat-head machine screw
3   ¼" wing nuts and washers
2   #6 x ¾" pan-head sheet metal screws
Optional self adhesive measuring tape
(right to left read style)
2" x 2" scrap of clear acrylic (Plexiglas)
Various wood screws, etc.

PART ONE: THE TABLE & FENCE

STEP 1: Use a router table to cut a pair of ¾"-wide slots in panel A. The slots should be deep enough for your T-track to fit inside flush with the surface of the panel. The slots should stop 18" from the panel's end. One slot should be in the center of the panel, the other ¾" from its edge as shown in **Figure 1**. Use a chisel to square the ends of the slots and mount a piece of T-track in each. You will have to file off the tips of the screws after you mount the track because they will poke through the other side.

STEP 2: Glue part B on the other face of panel A, along one of the edges. Then lay a piece of T-track against the edge of part B as shown in **Figure 2**. This will serve as a spacer as you mount part C to the face of the panel. You want the T-track to slide freely without any side-to-side wobble. This spacing is critical! The resulting slot shouldn't be too loose, or too tight **(Figure 3)**.

STEP 3: Lay a length of T-track down the center of panel D. Place panel A on top so that the T-track is in the slot with the first screw hole exposed as seen in **Figure 4**. Make sure that the edges of the panels are all aligned, then apply two clamps as illustrated. Carefully bore a pilot hole for a screw in the T-track. It is very important that the screw is exactly centered and driven in straight. Otherwise the tapered head will shift the T-track as it is tightened down. If one or more screws are off center down the length of the track, it will warp the track itself enough to effect the motion of the sliding table.

STEP 4: After the first screw is in place, loosen the clamps. Move the panel down to expose the next screw. Check to ensure that the panel's edges are aligned with the panel below it and reclamp. Bore your pilot hole and insert another screw. Repeat this process all down the length of the track.

Figure 1

Figure 2

Figure 3

Figure 4

STEP 5: Bore a ⁵⁄₁₆" hole through the center of the slot in the bottom of panel A. Countersink the hole on the top surface of the panel to fit the head of a ¼" machine screw. Insert a T-nut in the track and use the machine screw to secure the sliding portion of the table to the lower panel **(Figures 5 and 6)**. Leave the screw loose during sliding operations. Tighten it to lock the table.

STEP 6: Cut a 45° miter on one end of part BB, then use a ¼" bit in a router table to cut a slot down the center stopping the slot 2½" from the mitered end and 1" from the other end **(Figure 7)**.

STEP 7: Lay part AA on the bench as shown in **Figure 7.** Measure from the top left corner down the end of the part ¾", then draw a line at a 45° angle from that point to the other edge of the part. Cut along that line creating a blunted point.

STEP 8: Glue part BB on top of part Z so that their points meet as shown in **Figure 8**.

STEP 9: Attach a strip of T-track to the top edge of part AA as shown in **Figure 9**.

STEP 10: Clamp part Z to the face of your fence assembly as shown in **Figure 10**. This is a sacrificial face, so do not glue it in place. Instead, drive three screws through the side of the fence that is seen in the image to attach part Z.

STEP 11: Assemble parts X and Y as shown in **Figure 11**.

STEP 12: Place your new stop block on the fence as shown in **Figure 12**. Bore a hole ⁵⁄₁₆" in the top of part Y directly above the T-track beneath. Use a T-bolt, a washer and a wing nut to secure the stop.

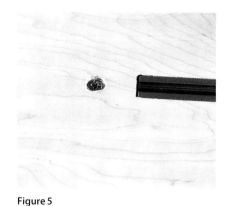

Figure 5

Figure 6

Figure 7

Figure 8

Figure 9

Figure 10

Figure 11

Figure 12

How Will You be Mounting Your Table?

If you are going to be building our Table Saw Workstation you're almost finished with this project already! The "base" portion of these plans is for those who wish to attach the sliding table to a stand-alone contractor or cabinet-style table saw.

Stumpy Nubs Woodworking
PRO TIP

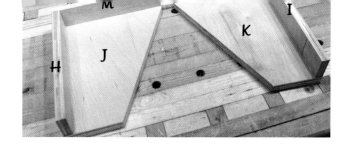

Figure 13

PART TWO: THE BASE

STEP 13: Lay part J on your bench with one of the shorter edges facing you. Measure from the bottom left corner up the side 1" and place a mark. Now measure from the upper right corner across the top edge 4½". Draw a line to connect those two points and cut along the line. Repeat this process with parts K and L as well (**Figure 13**).

STEP 14: Place part L on the bench in the position shown in **Figure 15**. Measure from the top left corner down the left edge, placing a mark at $2^{11}/_{16}$" and another at $10^{11}/_{16}$". Now use a square to draw lines from each of those two points to the right 3½". Connect the ends of the two lines forming a rectangle. Cut out the shape as shown in **Figure 13**.

STEP 15: Connect parts H, I, M and N to the face of parts J and K along their edges to create two brackets that are mirror images of each other as shown in **Figure 14**.

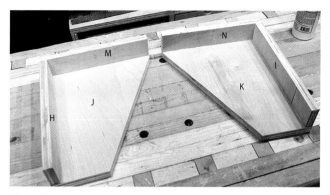

Figure 14

STEP 16: Attach parts E and F to the inside of the cutout in part L as shown in **Figure 15**. (Parts E and F are wider than the depth of the cutout so they will protrude above the edge of panel L.)

STEP 17: Attach the panel K assembly to the end of parts E and F as shown in **Figures 16 and 17**.

Figure 15

Figure 16

Which Way Does Your Saw Tilt?

The base of this unit is designed for saws with the tilt crank on the right side. If your saw has the crank on the left side, you will have to reverse the design of the base unit so it will mount on the other side of the saw. It's not that difficult; you just reverse the three brackets (J–L). The fence will have to be reversed as well. Generally, modern left-tilt saws will accept this design without modifications, but older saws may require it.

Stumpy Nubs Woodworking — PRO TIP

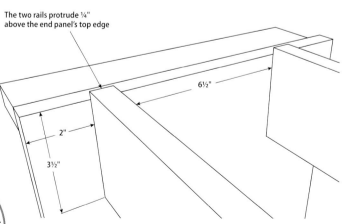

The two rails protrude ¼" above the end panel's top edge

6½"

2"

3½"

Figure 17

Figure 18

Figure 19

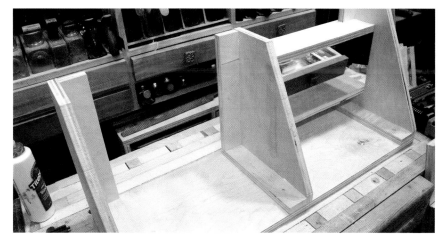

Figure 20

Figure 21

STEP 18: Attach parts O, P and Q to the inside face of panel L, on either side of the cutout as shown in **Figures 18 and 19**.

STEP 19: One handle threads into the micro-adjuster assembly on the top of the carriage (**Figure 19**) while the other fits beneath the fence (**Figure 25**). Epoxy ¼" acorn cap nuts on the ends of both handles after you install them.

STEP 20: Drive screws through the back of all three brackets (parts M, N and O) and into panel R as shown in **Figure 20**.

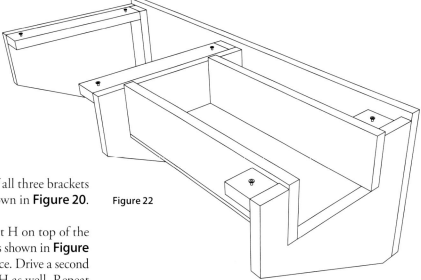

Figure 22

STEP 21: Drive a 1½" wood screw into part H on top of the rear bracket, about 2" from the back panel as shown in **Figure 21**. Leave the head about ½" above the surface. Drive a second screw about 1" from the other end of part H as well. Repeat the process with two more screws, one in each end of part I on the middle bracket. Finally drive a screw through the center of parts P and Q. These six screws (**Figure 22**) can be driven deeper, or backed out higher to adjust the level of the sliding table after it is mounted onto the side of your table saw. (See online content at stumpynubs.com/handmade-tools.html.)

Figure 23

Figure 24

Figure 26

Figure 25

Figure 27

STEP 22: After the assembly is mounted to your saw, and the sliding table portion is leveled with the top of the saw using the screws from the last step, you can drive six more screws from the bottom side of the brackets, up into the sliding table above it to secure it in place. It is best to position these screws right next to the leveling screws, though on the opposite face **(Figure 23)**.

STEP 23: The drawer front (part U) requires a ¾"-wide x ¼"-deep rabbet cut along both short edges, and a ¼"-wide rabbet along one of the long edges. This will provide a place to fit the ends of the two drawer side panels (S and T) as seen in **Figure 24**.

STEP 24: Attach the drawer back panel (V) between the two sides as shown in **Figure 25**.

STEP 25: Glue the drawer bottom panel in place as shown in **Figure 26**.

STEP 26: A second piece of ¼" MDF (part G) is attached to the bottom edges of parts E and F as shown in **Figure 27**.

STEP 27: You may also wish to attach a knob to the drawer front before inserting it into its place as shown in **Figure 28**.

Figure 28

STEP 28: If you will not be building our Table Saw Workstation you will have to mount the base assembly to the side of your table saw. This will require removing the wing on the left side of your saw. Get some help to hold the base assembly onto the side of the saw as shown in **Figure 29**. The top edge of the back panel (R) should be against the underside of the cast iron saw top. This will ensure that your sliding table is level with the top of the saw. Use several self tapping sheet metal screws to secure the assembly in place. You may choose to drill holes and use ¼" carriage bolts instead.

STEP 29: If you find that the unit is too heavy for your saw, you can add a leg to the front corner **(Figure 30)**.

STEP 30: Level the sliding table by raising or lowering the heads of the six adjustment screws in the top of the base assembly brackets **(Figure 31)**.

STEP 31: After the table is even with the top of the saw, drive screws through the underside of those brackets, near the leveling screws, up into the table above to secure it **(Figure 32)**.

NOTE: If you will be mounting your sliding crosscut table to the Table Saw Workstation, please refer to Chapter 12 for instructions.

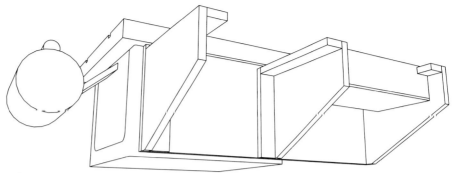

Figure 29

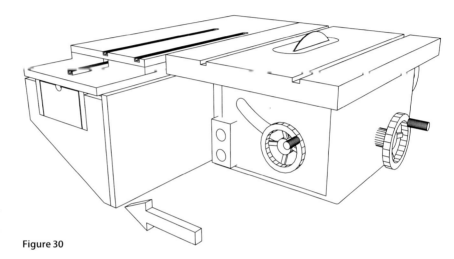

Figure 30

Figure 31

Figure 32

FREE ONLINE EXTRAS

The sliding crosscut table is a very accurate and safe way to cut everything from small parts to large panels. Learn how to get the most out of it by watching the free video content we've prepared for you on our website:
stumpynubs.com/homemade-tools/html

Table Saw Workstation

I love to organize things. Even as a child I would arrange my stuffed toys into groups based on size, color and personality. Everything had its place, and if someone had been in my room – or my office later in life (seven) – I could tell by the position of the things that had been touched. As I recall it, the doctors diagnosed me as having a severe case of crazy-nutjobitis. And by the doctors, I mean my parents.

This project appeals to my obsessive need to have the perfect place for everything, and it serves as a reminder that things aren't always as crazy as they seem. This book isn't just a haphazard collection of projects; they were all leading up to something. This is the chapter where everything comes together – where your homemade tools become a "homemade workshop!"

The Table Saw Workstation isn't just about the table saw – it's nearly an entire workshop in one little island no larger than a sheet of plywood. It upgrades your saw with the sliding crosscut table and homemade fence, incorporates our unique router table, adds the sanding and workholding benefits of the T-track downdraft table, and adds the curve cutting ability of our jigsaw. There's even a place to mount a lathe, a small drill press, a sharpening system or whatever other small tools you use most. And with 16 drawers and several shelves, you'll find room for hand-held power tools and supplies. There's even a built in lumber rack for cutoffs! Did I mention it's only 4' wide and 8' long? This isn't just a workstation; it's a mini-workshop. You can place it in the center of a shed, your basement, or even add some casters and roll it out of the way when someone wants to park their car in your garage workshop.

Due to the large number of steps in this project, you'll notice that instead of a materials list the chapter begins with diagrams that outline the cuts for the project. And there's no hardware list this time because it's pretty much limited to screws.

Don't feel like you have to build all of the projects in this book before you build the workstation. Just build the frame and extend the top to cover the whole thing. You can always cut portions of the top away should you choose to insert a tool later on. It's time to build the work space you always wanted, so let's get started!

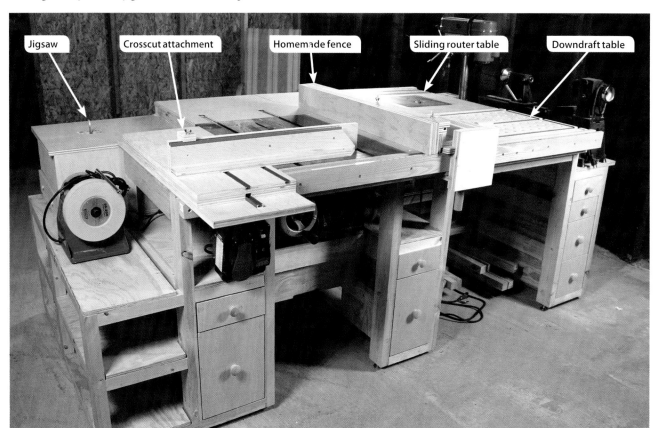

Everything comes together with this mini workshop in a 4' x 8' footprint!

Table Saw Workstation

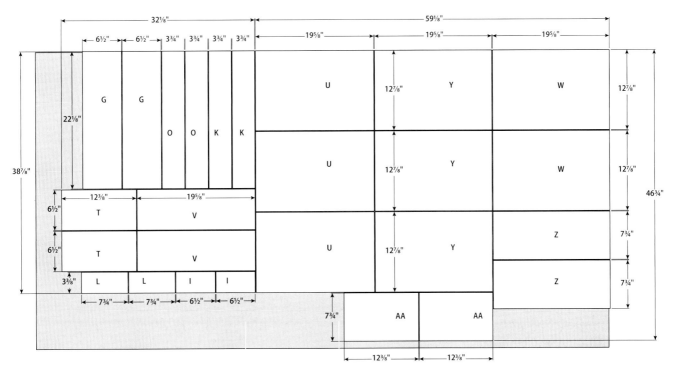

½" Plywood sheet #1

½" Plywood sheet #2

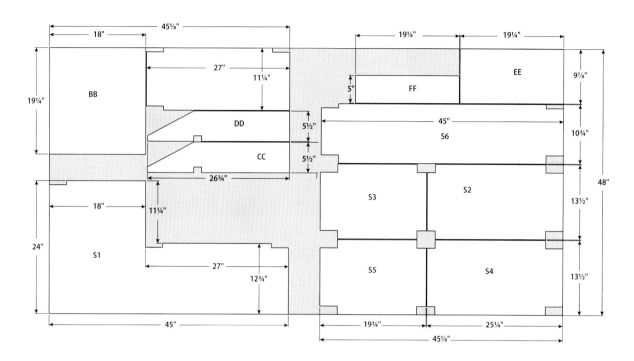

½" Plywood sheet #3

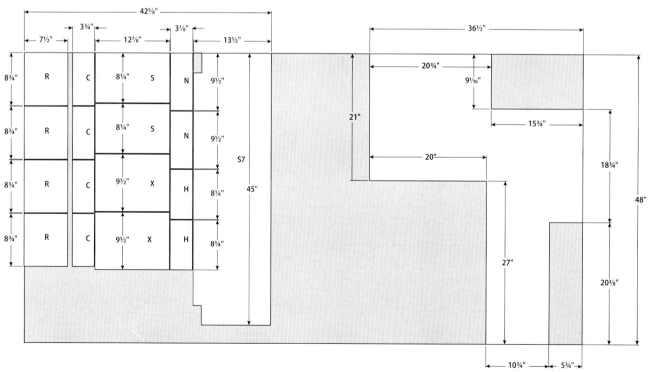

½" Plywood sheet #4

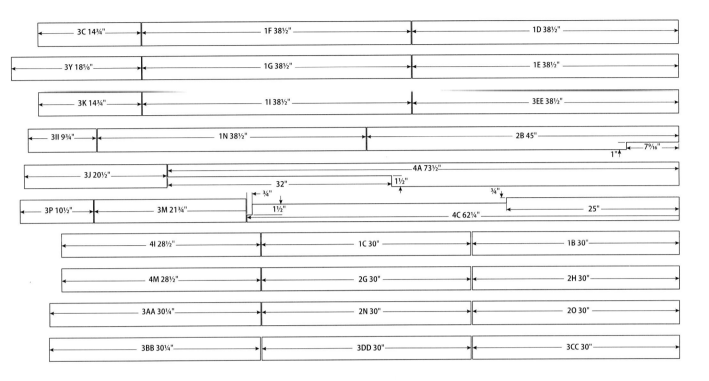

2 x 4 layout #1

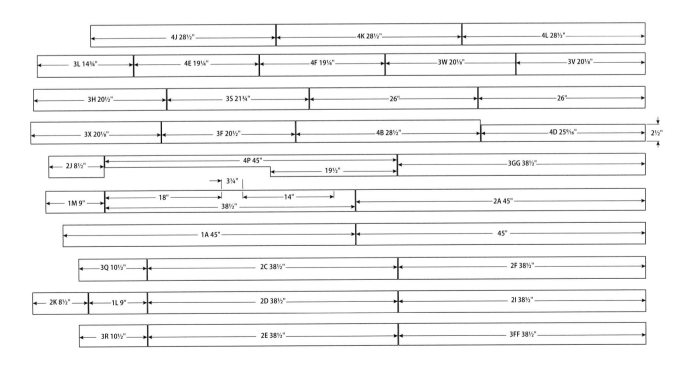

2 x 4 layout #2

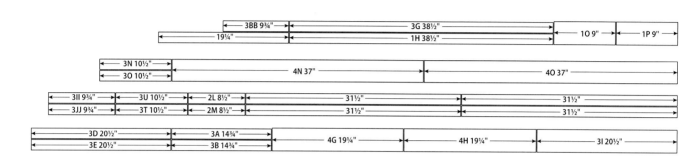

2 x 4 layout #3

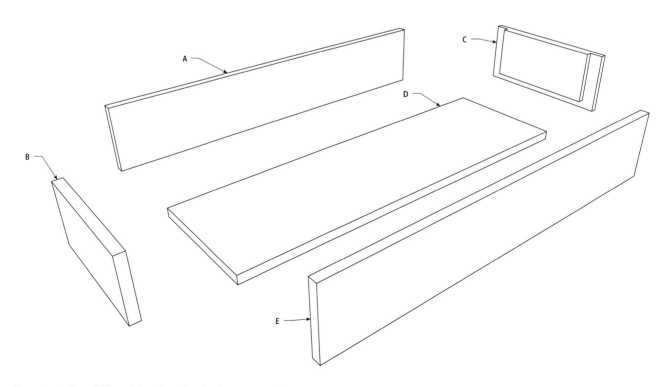

Drawer Size #1 (Build four of these based on the dimensions in the plywood diagrams)

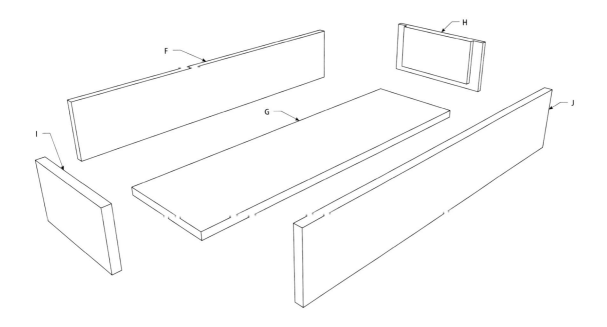

Drawer Size #2 (Build four of these based on the dimensions in the plywood diagrams)

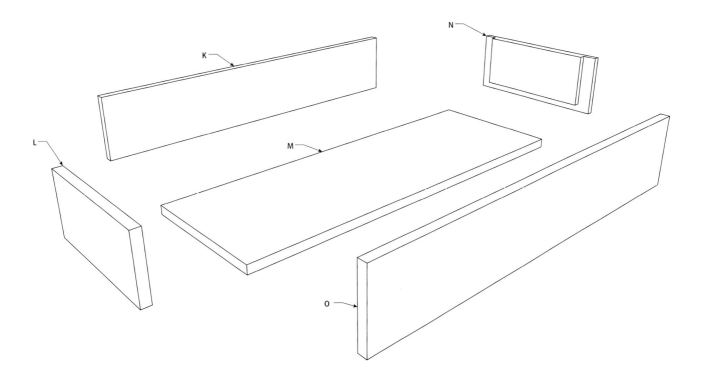

Drawer Size #3 (Build two of these based on the dimensions in the plywood diagrams)

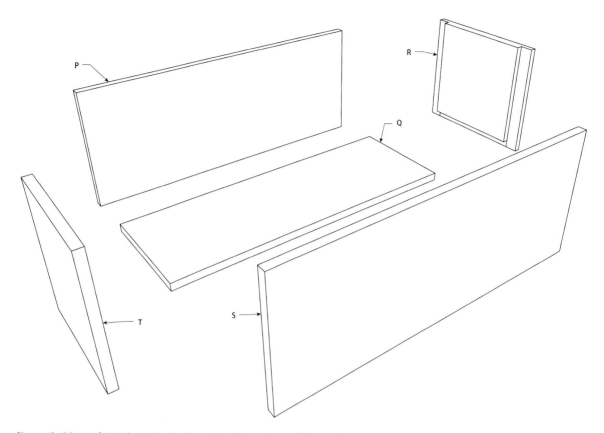

Drawer Size #4 (Build two of these based on the dimensions in the plywood diagrams)

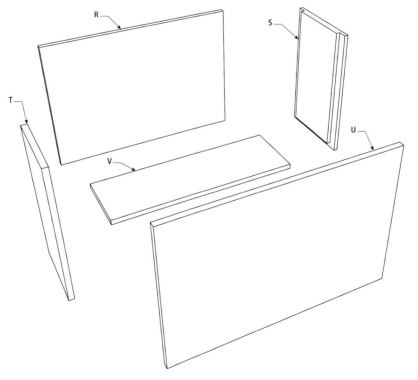

Drawer Size #5 (Build two of these based on the dimensions in the plywood diagrams)

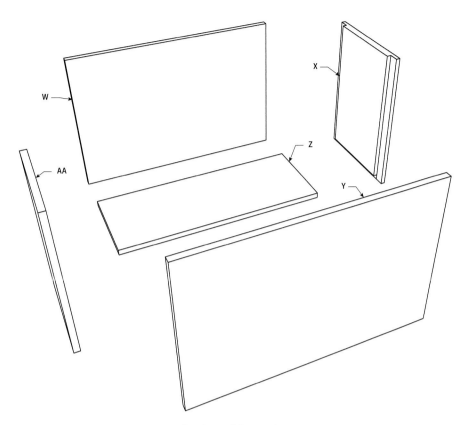

Drawer Size #6 (Build two of these based on the dimensions in the plywood diagrams)

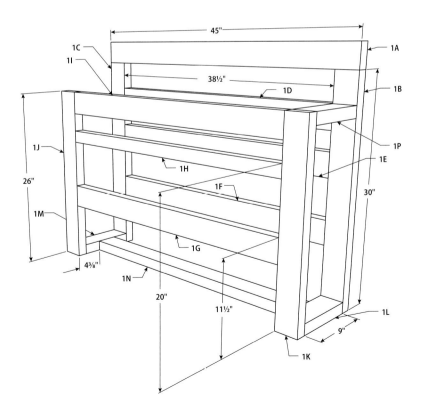

Frame Section One

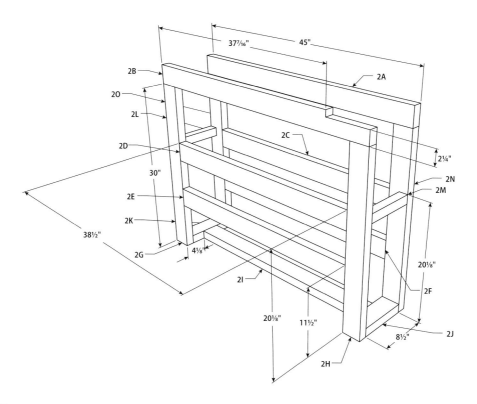

Frame Section Two

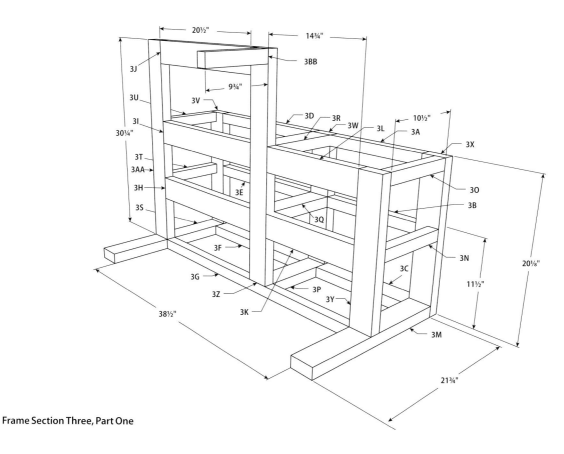

Frame Section Three, Part One

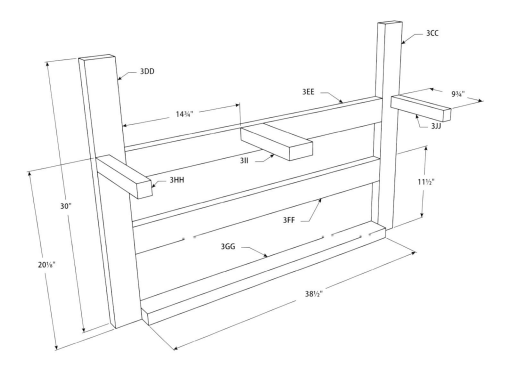

Frame Section Three, Part Two

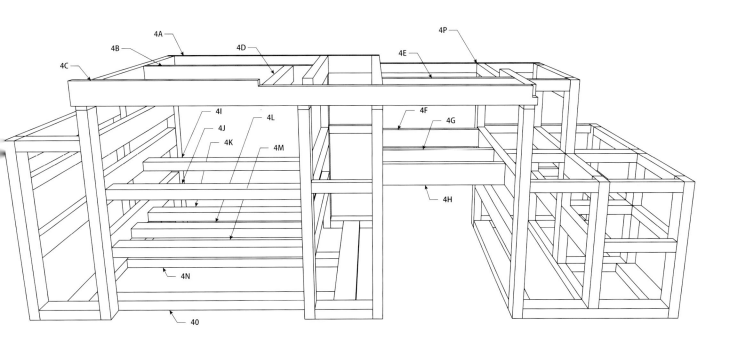

Frame Connecting Parts

PART ONE: THE DRAWERS

There are six drawer sizes in this project, but they are all constructed in the same way and from the same materials. The fronts are ¾" plywood while the rest of the parts are ½". We'll walk through the process of building one drawer, then you can apply the same steps to complete all 16.

STEP 1: Regardless of size, the drawer fronts all require rabbets along three of the four edges. The rabbet on the bottom edges is are ½" wide and ⅜" deep, while the rabbets on the sides are ⅞" wide and ⅜" deep. I strongly suggest you cut and rabbet all of your 16 drawer fronts at once so you won't be changing your saw or router table setups between drawers **(Figure 1)**.

STEP 2: The drawer sides are now attached to the front. Apply glue to both mating surfaces when you insert the end of the side panel into the rabbet **(Figure 2)**. Drive nails into the side of the drawer front to secure the side **(Figure 3)**.

STEP 3: Set the partial drawer on your bench with the bottom up. The drawer backs are ½" shorter than the sides. Glue and nail them between the drawer sides as shown in **Figure 4**.

STEP 4: Glue and nail the bottom panel in place as shown in **Figures 5 and 6**. That's all there is to it. Refer to **Figures 7-10** for more detailed images of how the drawers go together.

Figure 1

Figure 2

Figure 3

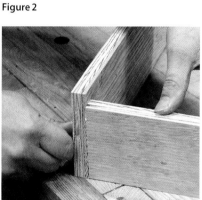
Figure 4

Figure 5

Figure 6

Figure 7

Figure 8

Figure 9

Figure 10

Easy-peasy Drawers

There certainly are stronger ways to build drawers, but I find this method to be very fast, easy and remarkably strong. The brad nails would have to shear in two for the front to pull off or the bottom to fall out. But, if you want to take the time to dovetail all of the drawers – have at it! Just remember, you will have to modify the sizes of the parts first.

PART TWO:
FRAME SECTION ONE

STEP 5: Even though we will build the frame one section at a time, you should take the time to cut all of your 2x4 parts using the provided diagrams. As you work is it very helpful to label every part with on the end so you will be able to easily locate them later. After cutting your parts to length (**Figure 10**), put a good blade in your table saw and rip each one to 3⅜" wide. Then place the freshly cut edge against the fence and run them all again, ripping them to the final width of 3¼". (There are also some 1½"-wide strips on the cutting diagram.)

STEP 6: All of the frame parts are held together with pocket screws. If you don't have a jig, I strongly suggest investing in at least an inexpensive version. If you examine the provided diagrams carefully you can see which ends of which parts will require holes. This will enable you to do a lot of the work ahead of the assembly (**Figure 11**).

STEP 7: Lay part 1J and 1K on the bench and attach parts L and M on the ends at 90° as shown in **Figure 12**.

STEP 8: Attach parts 1O and 1P to the other end of your parts in the same way as shown in **Figure 13**.

STEP 9: Attach your three part assemblies to parts 1B and 1C shown in **Figure 14**. Be sure parts 1O and 1P are squared!

STEP 10: Attach part 1F to one part 1B on one of your two assemblies. The edge of part F indicated by the arrow in **Figure 15** is 11½" from the bottom of the assembly indicated by the other arrow.

Figure 11

Figure 12

Figure 13

Figure 14

Figure 15

Figure 16

Figure 17

Figure 18

Figure 19

STEP 11: Attach part 1D to the junction as shown in **Figure 16**.

STEP 12: Attach parts 1G and 1I to part 1K directly across from the parts you just mounted as shown in **Figure 17**.

STEP 13: Attach the other assembly (made up of parts 1C, 1O, 1J and 1M) as shown in **Figure 18**. Be sure everything is square as you connect the ends of each piece.

STEP 14: Attach part 1N between parts 1L and 1M as shown in **Figure 19**.

STEP 15: Mount part 1H between parts 1J and 1K as shown in **Figure 20**. The top edge (indicated with an arrow) should be 20" from the bottom of the assembly. You need not insert the drawers at this time.

STEP 16: Mount part 1E between parts 1B and 1C as shown in **Figure 21**. The top edge (indicated with an arrow) should be 20" from the bottom of the assembly.

Figure 20

Figure 21

PART THREE: FRAME SECTION TWO

STEP 17: Lay parts 2G, 2H, 2N and 2O on your bench as shown in **Figure 22.** The bottom ends of the parts should be on your right. Draw a line across all four parts 1¹/₁₂" from the bottom ends. Draw another line 20 ⅛" from that same end.

STEP 18: Attach part 2J to the bottom end of 2N, and part 2K to the bottom end of 2O as shown in **Figure 23.**

STEP 19: Attach parts 2M and 2L to parts 2N and 2O as shown in **Figure 24**. They should be mounted just to the right of the line farthest from the ends.

STEP 20: Attach parts 2G and 2H to create two assemblies as shown in **Figure 25**.

STEP 21: Attach part 2I to one of the assemblies, centered on the bottom as shown in **Figure 26**.

STEP 22: Attach parts 2C and 2F as shown in **Figure 27**. Both should be on the bottom side of the lines you drew earlier.

STEP 23: Attach parts 2D and 2E directly across from 2C and 2F as shown in **Figure 28**.

STEP 24: Finally, connect the other assembly as shown in **Figure 29**.

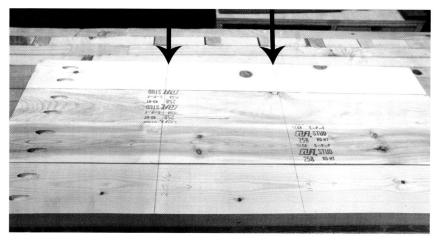

Figure 22

Figure 23

Figure 24

Figure 25

Figure 26

Figure 27

Figure 28

Figure 29

PART FOUR: FRAME SECTION THREE

STEP 25: Because this section is so complex, the provided diagrams are in two parts. But we'll be building it as a single unit. Begin by laying parts 3CC and 3DD on your bench as shown in **Figure 30**. This time, the ends to your left will be considered the bottom of the parts. Measure from those ends 11½" and 20⅛", drawing a line across both at those points.

STEP 26: Flip on part 3CC around on the bench so that the bottom end is facing away from you and attach parts 3EE and 3FF to the edge of 3CC, just to the bottom side of the lines you drew **(Figure 31)**.

STEP 27: Fasten part 3DD to the other end of 3EE and 3FF as shown in **Figure 32**.

STEP 28: Rotate the entire assembly so that the bottom side is now facing you and attach part 3GG between the ends as shown in **Figure 33**. Notice that 3GG is rotated 90°.

STEP 29: Attach part 3M to the junction as shown in **Figure 34**. Attach part 3AA in the same way on in the junction on the opposite end of part 3GG.

STEP 30: Flip the entire assembly on end so that part 3GG is flat on the bench as shown in **Figure 35**. Attach part 3Y so that the edge indicated by the arrow in 10½" from the end closest to you (also indicated by an arrow).

STEP 31: Measure up part 3Y 10" and draw a line. Attach part 3N at that point, below the line as shown in **Figure 36**.

STEP 32: Fasten part 30 to the top of 3Y as shown in **Figure 37**.

Figure 30

Figure 31

Figure 32

Figure 33

Figure 34

Figure 35

Figure 36

Figure 37

Figure 38

Figure 39

STEP 33: Attach part 3X to the to the ends of parts 3O, 3N and 3M as shown in **Figure 38**. Be sure the horizontal parts are squared!

STEP 34: Measure from the end of part EE (indicated by the arrow in **Figure 39**) 14¾" and draw a line. Attach part 3JJ to the right of that line as shown in **Figure 39**.

STEP 35: Attach part 3MM just below the line you previously drew on part 3CC as shown in **Figure 40**.

STEP 36: Attach part 3AA as shown in **Figure 41**. The lower end of 3AA fastens on top of part 3S **(Figure 42)**.

STEP 37: Attach part 3G between the junctions in parts 3M and 3S as shown in **Figure 42**.

Figure 40

Figure 41

Figure 42

Figure 43

Figure 44

STEP 38: Attach part 3Z as shown in **Figure 43**. Use a square to check all of your parts before fastening.

STEP 39: Measure from the top ends of parts 3AA and 3Z 9⅞" and 18½", placing a mark at both points (**Figure 44**).

STEP 40: Attach 3J at the top between parts 3AA and 3Z, then part 3I just below your upper line, and finally 3H below the lower line as shown in **Figure 44**.

Figure 45

Figure 46

STEP 41: Attach part 3L between 3Y and 3Z as shown in **Figure 45**.

STEP 42: Fasten part 3P to the junction of parts 3G and 3Z as shown in **Figure 46**.

STEP 43: Attach part 3K just below the line on part 3Z as shown in **Figure 47**.

Figure 47

STEP 44: Fasten the bottom end of part 3W to the end of part 3P as shown **Figure 48**.

STEP 45: Attach part 3D at the top between 3W and 3X, then fasten part 3E below it at the same level as 3N on the end of your assembly as shown in **Figure 48**.

Figure 48

Figure 49

STEP 46: Attach the lower end of part 3V to the end of 3S, then place 3T between 3V and 3AA just below the line you drew previously as shown in **Figure 49**.

STEP 47: Attach part 3U at the top of 3V as shown in **Figure 49**.

STEP 48: Attach parts 3C and 3F at the bottom of the assembly as shown in **Figure 50**.

STEP 49: Attach part 3J to the top of the assembly as shown in **Figure 51**.

Figure 50

Figure 51

Figure 52

Figure 53

PART FIVE:
MOUNTING THE DRAWERS

STEP 50: Rather than spending a small fortune for drawer slides, I opted to make some simple hardwood sliders. However, I designed the drawers with ½" of clearance on each side, so if you prefer something smoother you may use ball-bearing drawer slides. Otherwise, rip a bunch of hardwood strips that are ½" x ¾". You'll need 32 of them that are 20" long and eight that are 18½" long. All of the lower drawers have no slides.

STEP 51: The key to the drawers is simply locating the slides on the parts of the frame that are closest to each drawer. Do one section of the frame at a time. Begin by using a square to mark lines showing the location of your horizontal rails. Carry these lines all the way to the front face of each vertical post so you can see them with the drawers in place (**Figure 52**).

Figure 54

STEP 52: Insert the drawers placing ⅛"-thick spacers between each front panel as shown in **Figure 53**.

STEP 53: Locate the position of the drawer slides by carrying the line that indicates the edge of the nearest rail onto the face of the drawer. If the bottom edge of the rail is closest to the center of your drawer, then mark a second line ¾" above it on the drawer face. Mark an "X" above that line. This is the location that you will carry down the side of the drawer to position the slide. Mark a second "X" above the line on the post. This will remind you that the portion of the slide that fastens to the rail is located below the slide on the drawer.

NOTE: if the top edge of the rail is nearest the center of your drawer, you will simply carry the line from your post to your drawer front, then place an "X" above the line on the drawer, and below the line of the post. No need to measure ¾" (**Figure 53**). The idea is to fasten the lower strip of each slide either along the top or bottom edge of the nearest rail so it is easy to keep them parallel. Then you mount the upper strip of each slide above that position on the side of the drawer.

Figure 55

STEP 54: Use glue and nails to fasten the wooden strips inside the carcase. The front end of each strip should be positioned ⅜" from the front edge of each post to leave room for the drawer fronts. Remember to match the length of the strips to the drawers. The third row down on frame section one is short drawers, as are all bottom drawers (**Figure 55**).

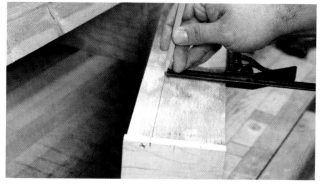
Figure 56

Figure 57

Figure 58

Figure 59

STEP 55: Use a combination square to carry your locating line from the drawer front panels down the sides (**Figure 56**).

STEP 56: Glue and nail the strips to the drawers (**Figure 57**).

STEP 57: The bottom drawers do not get runners, but you should glue scraps of wood as stops ⅜" from the edges of the posts where the drawer front will hit them (**Figure 56**).

Repeat steps 50-57 for all of the drawers. Label your drawers so you can easily match them to their place in the frame!

STEP 58: Simple leg levels are well worth the investment rather than shimming the legs of your bench to level the top later. These levelers are installed by boring a hole into the bottom of the posts to receive the bolt end. They can then be adjusted with a wrench. I installed four levelers on each of the three frame sections (**Figure 61 and 62**).

STEP 59: Position all three frame sections as shown in **Figure 63**. Don't worry about accurate spacing yet.

STEP 60: Three rails connect sections two and three and support the table saw. Measuring from the side of the frame indicated with the arrow in **Figure 63**, mount 4F 4¼" in, 4G 22¼" in and 4H 32½" in.

Figure 60

Figure 61

Figure 62

Figure 63

What's Up With the Short Drawers?

Hardwood sliders will last longer than you will. Just apply some beeswax once in a while to keep them sliding smoothly. You've likely noticed that some of the drawers are shorter than others. Why is this? It's to leave room to run 4" PVC ducts for adding dust collection to your workstation. We won't get into that in this chapter, but if you do decide to add dust collection, be sure to check out the video on our website that will walk you through it:
stumpynubs.com/homemade-tools/html

Figure 64

Figure 65

Figure 66

STEP 61: If your saw doesn't have a lower dust panel already installed, now is the time to assemble the optional dust shield shown in **Figure 69**. Use that diagram to cut the shape of the side panels (CC and DD).

STEP 62: Cut a hole in the bottom panel (BB) to fit a 4" blast gate. Drive screws from inside the blast gate, through the plastic and into the edge of the plywood panel **(Figure 65)**.

STEP 63: All of the dust panel's parts can be assembled with glue except part FF, which is attached with screws to provide access to the inside for cleaning out if needed **(Figure 66)**.

Figure 67

STEP 64: The end of the blast gate will have to be cut off flush with the inner face of the bottom panel **(Figure 67)**. You can do so in place with a saw; or mark it with a felt-tip pen, remove the blast gate to cut, and reinstall after trimming. Then caulk around the seams. Do not caulk the removable panel (FF).

STEP 65: Install the dust panel assembly from the bottom of your partially assembled frame, so tip it up on its edge. The notches in the sides (indicated by the arrows in **Figure 68**) should slip over rail 4G, allowing the sides of the assembly to be screwed to the inner faces of rails 2C and 3EE.

Figure 68

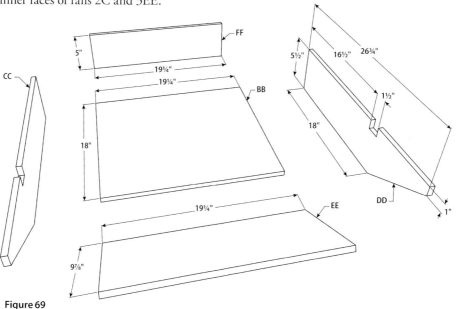

Figure 69

Figure 70

Figure 71

Figure 72

Figure 73

STEP 66: Rail 4P requires some extra work. Raise your saw blade ¾" above the table and set your fence 1¾" from the blade. Cut a kerf into one face of the part all the way down its length. Use a pencil to place an "X" on the edge of the part that was against the fence. Reset your blade to 1½". Run the part through again, this time with the edge you marked with an "X" facing up. Discard the strip of waste that results. Position the part as shown in **Figure 70**. Measure 19½" inches from the end closest to you, then cut away the thin portion of the part from that point to the opposite end. The part should now look like **Figure 70**.

STEP 67: Get someone to help you set your table saw in place as shown **Figure 71**, then mount rail 4P on top of posts 3CC and 3DD as shown. Part 3BB also mounts between posts 3Z and rail 4P as shown in **Figure 71**. The saw's top should be at the same level as the top edge of rail 4P. Shim beneath the saw as needed to achieve that height.

NOTE: During the course of this project we experimented with a rear dust shield assembly (marked with an "X" in **Figure 71**) which worked well, but prevented the saw's motor from fully tilting. Because of this limitation we did away with it.

STEP 68: Attach rail 2A to the top of the posts on the other side of the saw as shown in **Figure 72**. If the saw's top is not level with the top edge of this rail as well, shim beneath the saw as needed.

STEP 69: Cut a 1½" x 7⁹⁄₁₆" notch from the end of rail 2B, then install it to the top of the posts as shown in **Figure 73**.

STEP 70: You will also have to modify rail 4C. Set your table saw fence 2½" from the blade. Rip a kerf in the rail, stopping 25" short of the end as shown in **Figure 74**. Use a handsaw to finish removing the thin strip of waste.

STEP 71: Measure from the narrower of the two ends in ¾" and place a mark on the freshly cut edge of the rail. Draw a line from that point 1½" toward the opposite edge, then carry it at a right angle back to the end of the rail. Use a handsaw to cut on the two lines leaving a 1" x ¾" tab on the rail's end (**Figure 75**).

Figure 74

Figure 75

Figure 76

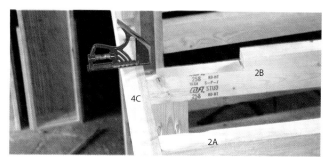

Figure 77

Figure 78

STEP 72: Rail 4C can now be mounted to your frame assembly. The notched end should be screwed to rail 4P (drill a pilot hole first!) as shown in **Figure 76**. Set a combination square to ¾" to ensure that the top edge of rail 4C is the proper height above the notch in rail 2B **(Figure 77)**. Drive screws into the ends of both 2B and 2A.

STEP 73: Rail 1A can now be mounted to top of section one of your frame. It attaches to the top of posts 1B and 1C. Then the end of rail 4C attaches to the end of 1A as shown in **Figure 78**. Note that rail 1A is ¾" lower than 4C **(Figure 79)**.

STEP 74: Parts 4I and 4J are the router table supports. They attach between rails 1E of frame section one, and 2D of frame section two. Position them so that their ends are at aligned with the bottom edges of the rails and use pocket screws driven from the top faces to secure them. 4I should be mounted 20½" from the face of the frame assembly **(Figure 80)**.

STEP 75: Parts 4K, 4L and 4M are to be mounted in the same way, except one level lower between rails 1F and 2E. 4K should be mounted 20½" from the face of the frame assembly. The rest don't matter **(Figure 80)**.

STEP 76: Parts 4N and 4O are mounted between rails 1N and the bottom of frame section one, and 2I at the bottom of frame section two. 4K should be also mounted 20½" from the face of the frame assembly **(Figure 80)**.

Figure 79

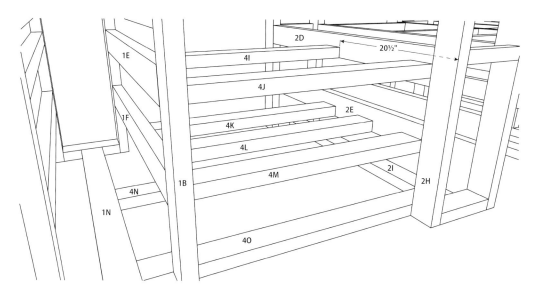

Figure 80

STEP 77: Rail 4A requires a long notch similar to the one you cut in 4C. Set your table saw fence 2" from the blade and rip a 32"-long kerf in one end. Use a handsaw to finish removing the thin strip of waste. Mount the rail across all three sections of your frame assembly as seen in **Figure 81**.

STEP 78: Position part 4E between rails 2A and 4P, 7" from 4C as shown in **Figure 81**.

STEP 79: Position part 4B between rails 1A and 2B, 25 9/16" from 4C as shown in **Figure 81**.

STEP 80: Part 4D must be ripped down to 2½" wide, then mounted between rails 4C and 4B, 23¾" from 1A as shown in **Figure 81**. Note that one end is flush with the notch in 4C and the other end is flush with the top edge of 4B.

STEP 81: If you are mounting our homemade Sliding Top Router Table into your workstation, set it into the opening between rails 1A and 4D, on top of parts 4I and 4J as seen in **Figure 82**. You will have to shorten the rear overhang of the router table by sawing off 35/16". The remaining rear overhang will rest on top of rail 4B. Shim beneath the table as needed so that the front top of the router table is level with the top edge of rail 4C.

STEP 82: Cut the top panel from ¾" plywood. The dimensions given in **Figure 83** are not necessarily the same ones you will need. Your table saw may be a different size, or you may choose not to build the downdraft table or router table. Place whatever inserts you plan to use in the saw frame and then measure for your top panel. (The "removable insert" panel is only needed if you are using the sliding router table.)

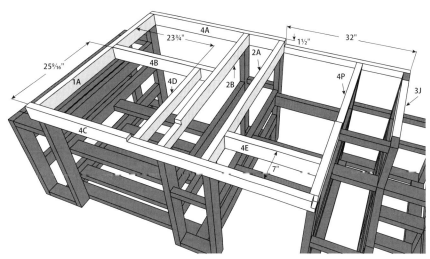

Figure 81

Figure 82

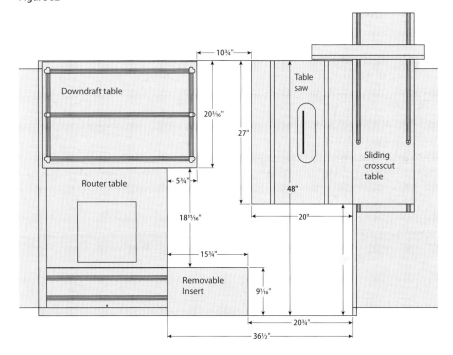

Figure 83

Figure 84

Figure 85

Figure 86

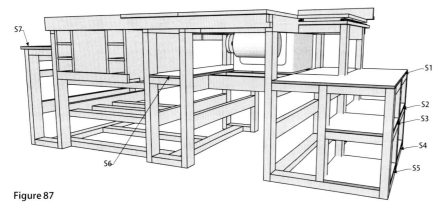

Figure 87

Figure 88

STEP 83: Lay the top panel in place. Mark the location of your table saw's miter slots, then use a router to carry those slots across about 8" across the table top as seen in **Figure 84**.

STEP 84: Shim beneath the machines, adjust your leg levelers, or shim beneath the top as needed to get everything on the same plane, then fasten the top down with screws around the entire perimeter **(Figure 85)**.

STEP 85: Place all of the shelf panels **(Figure 87)**, using screws or nails to secure them. **NOTE:** Some of the panels will have to be ripped down the center because they will not fit between the frame components **(Figure 86)**.

STEP 86: Insert all of the drawers in their places. Hopefully you labeled them so this process is easier! You may wish to add some drawer pulls to the fronts as well.

STEP 87: In order for the sliding portion of the router table to operate you will need a removable insert in the main benchtop panel **(Figure 83)**. Cut a scrap of ¾" plywood to fit inside the opening, placing it on the notched portions of the rails below. Cut a second scrap to fit in the opening in the top panel. Attach the two together as seen in **Figure 88**.

STEP 88: If you will be installing the sliding table option, now is the time to mount it. Place both layers onto the frame to the left of the table saw. Use a straightedge as you shim beneath the lower sliding table panel until it is on the same plane as the table saw's top **(Figure 89)**.

Figure 89

Figure 90

STEP 89: Remove the upper half of the sliding table and drive screws through the lower panel to secure it to the frame below. Be sure to countersink the screw heads **(Figure 90)**.

STEP 90: Add a little beeswax to the top of the lower table and the T-track, then replace the upper portion.

ONLINE CONTENT

This workstation was designed to accommodate several of our homemade woodworking tools including the T-track downdraft table, the sliding router table and the jigsaw. We've produced some extra video of the whole thing in action, which you can watch for free on our website: **stumpynubs.com/homemade-tools/html**

The Homemade Workshop, Copyright © 2015 by James Hamilton. Printed and bound in U.S.A. All rights reserved. No part of this book may be reproduced in any form or by any electronic or mechanical means including information storage and retrieval systems without permission in writing from the publisher, except by a reviewer, who may quote brief passages in a review. Published by Popular Woodworking Books, an imprint of F+W, A Content + eCommerce Company, 10151 Carver Rd. Blue Ash, Ohio, 45242. First edition.

Distributed in Canada by Fraser Direct
100 Armstrong Avenue
Georgetown, Ontario L7G 5S4
Canada

Distributed in the U.K. and Europe by
F+W Media International, LTD
Brunel House, Ford Close
Newton Abbot
Devon TQ12 4PU, UK
Tel: (+44) 1626 323200
Fax: (+44) 1626 323319

Distributed in Australia by Capricorn Link
P.O. Box 704
Windsor, NSW 2756
Australia

Visit our website at popularwoodworking.com or our consumer website at shopwoodworking.com for more woodworking information.

Other fine Popular Woodworking Books are available from your local bookstore or direct from the publisher.

ISBN-13: 978-1-4403-4166-3

19 18 17 16   5 4 3 2

Editor: *Scott Francis*
Designer: *Angela Wilcox*
Copy Editor: *Megan Fitzpatrick*
Production Coordinator: *Debbie Thomas*

a content + ecommerce company

Read This Important Safety Notice

To prevent accidents, keep safety in mind while you work. Use the safety guards installed on power equipment. When working on power equipment, keep fingers away from saw blades, wear safety goggles to prevent injuries from flying wood chips and sawdust, wear hearing protection and consider installing a dust vacuum to reduce the amount of airborne sawdust in your woodshop. Don't wear loose clothing or jewelry when working on power equipment. Tie back long hair to prevent it from getting caught in your equipment. People who are sensitive to certain chemicals should check the chemical content of any product before using it. The authors and editors who compiled this book have tried to make the contents as accurate and correct as possible. Plans, illustrations, photographs and text have been carefully checked. All instructions, plans and projects should be carefully read, studied and understood before beginning construction. Due to the variability of local conditions, construction materials, skill levels, etc., neither the author nor Popular Woodworking Books assumes any responsibility for any accidents, injuries, damages or other losses incurred resulting from the material presented in this book. Prices listed for supplies and equipment were current at the time of publication and are subject to change.

Metric Conversion Chart

Inches	Centimeters	2.54
Centimeters	Inches	0.4
Feet	Centimeters	30.5
Centimeters	Feet	0.03
Yards	Meters	0.9
Meters	Yards	1.1

Ideas • Instruction • Inspiration

Receive FREE downloadable bonus materials when you sign up for our FREE newsletter at **popularwoodworking.com**.

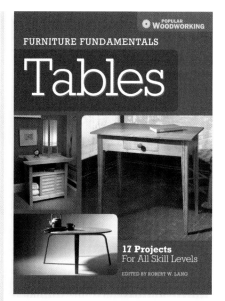

Find the latest issues of *Popular Woodworking Magazine* on newsstands, or visit **popularwoodworking.com**.

These and other great Popular Woodworking products are available at your local bookstore, woodworking store or online supplier. Visit our website at **shopwoodworking.com**.

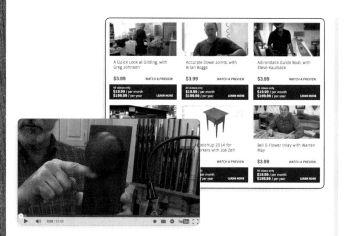

Visit our Website

Find helpful and inspiring articles, videos, blogs, projects and plans at **popularwoodworking.com**.

For behind the scenes information, become a fan at **Facebook.com/popularwoodworking**.

For more tips, clips and articles, follow us at **twitter.com/pweditors**.

For visual inspiration, follow us at **pinterest.com/popwoodworking**.

Popular Woodworking Videos

Subscribe and get immediate access to the web's best woodworking subscription site. You'll find more than 400 hours of woodworking video tutorials and full-length video workshops from world-class instructors on workshops, projects, SketchUp, tools, techniques and more!

videos.popularwoodworking.com

For free videos visit **youtube.com/popwoodworking**.